Starting from Scratch

More Stories About Siamese Cat Rescue

by

BARBARA GALIN

TATTERSALL PUBLISHING

Book Design and Layout by
Crystal Wood/Tattersall Publishing
www.tattersallpub.com

ISBN 978-1-7320129-0-5

On the Cover: Pi, aka Moon Pie *(see page 48)*

Table of Contents

Dedication v

Acknowledgments vii

Introduction to Cat Behavior ix

The Stories

Andrew, the Lazy Susan Cat 1

Frankie Blue Eyes 6

Annie with the White Sneakers 13

The Neighbors' Cat, Azul 16

Siamese Rescue—To the Rescue! 20

New Beginnings:
    Momma Penny with Linc and Zelda 25

Whitney's Story..30

Spike's Journey 36

Taking a Chance on Lucy..41

Empty Hallways...45

Pi, AKA Moon Pie 48

Yule..50

Lily...52

Wren and Whitaker...54

Jim Bob, AKA Theo 60

The Story of Velvet and Bandit.................................63

Zeus and the Pills..68

Oliver...70

Duchess..73

Sinda..75

You Are My Sunshine..79

Five Brothers 82

Sometimes You Just Need A Leg Up in Life.............91

Rudy's Story 94
Allsa, AKA Harvey 97
Mojo Rising 100
The Snowshoe Sisters.....................................104
Newbury 107
Peter the Cat 110

Dedication

To Brandy Bear and all the rescue cats
whose stories continue to live in my head and heart.

Acknowledgments

*T*his book is a history of sorts. It is written to honor the cat rescuers, adopters and the cats themselves whose stories I choose to share with others. Some of the stories are mine and others have been contributed by my friend and co-rescuer Mary Pelchat, who I have worked with for many years rescuing Siamese Cats. Still other stories have been included from others to show the dedication of the many people who care so deeply for these special loving animals. It is not just one person who steps up to make a difference. It is the work of many who work together to put miracles into motion and get the job done. I am blessed to have had a part in that journey.

Thank you, Mary and Judith, for all your editing work.

Thank you to my husband, who lives the life of a foster husband. He still yells to me from the bedroom, "When are you coming to bed? Are you staying in the foster room tonight?" He is more heartbroken each time one of the foster cats goes home than I am. I am always nervous the first couple of days after a foster cat has left but then I know in my heart that if Siamese Rescue did its job correctly, this cat is in the best possible responsible and loving home. After twenty years you would think my husband has some wonderful stories to tell. He tells me no, he does not remember any one foster. I guess after more than eighty foster cats it can get blurred but I don't believe him for one minute.

Thank you to my son Matt, who cannot come to my home to visit with his wife Kristi and my grandkids without sneezing and wheezing. When I started this journey by adopting my first Siamese cat, Jasmine, and then Chelsea, in 1990, Matt and I both got allergy shots to control our allergies to cats. The shots worked to desensitize me and Matt while he lived at home, but that was many years ago. I think he now realizes that rescue has become my extended family and my saving grace.

And lastly, thank you to the rescue community that works so hard to save just one life at a time and then many more. It is hard and unforgiving work and I am humbled and honored to know you.

Barbara Galin, volunteer for Siamese Cat Rescue, VA

Introduction to Cat Behavior

Siamese cats have been my passion for over twenty years, with the majority of those years volunteering for Siamese Rescue, which is a cat breed rescue. Their beauty and quirky personality make me fall in love with them over and over. I am sure there are other breeds just as dear to their guardians, but because Siamese cats have gone through my home and heart for over twenty years I call them special. They are my comfort, my therapy, and my way of making a small difference in this world. As a rescue community these cats make an enormous impact on our lives.

Some rescue cats arrive filled with loss and grief, bewilderment and fear. Others arrive with anger, while others just come with their tails held high.

I have learned an enormous amount about the how, what, when and why of the behavior of Siamese cats. While every cat is unique, there are qualities which give us insight to why a behavior happens. Most cats come into rescue without us knowing their history. It is the job of the person taking on the cat, i.e. the foster, to try and figure out what that history could possibly be. The knowledge gained helps to place the cat in the right environment at his/her future home. By telling the stories of the cats I have had the privilege of helping through rescue and the stories of other volunteers, I hope to help the prospective adopters and new rescue people understand and accept the different traits and personalities of Siamese cats.

The Alpha Cat – BIG PERSONALITY

The alpha cat is the cat that comes right out of the carrier to say "hi" in most situations. They immediately will show their strength and confidence. These cats may also be the ones to have issues with getting along with other cats in their homes by acting out. They might spray or bite when they are unhappy. They will not settle for being number two with their people and other pets. They can be jealous and/or territorial, but they can be the most loving and often are "Velcro®" cats who want to be in the middle of everything going on in the household. If you have an alpha personality cat, you cannot be a softy. You need to be "THE MAMMA" cat and let them know what is and what is not acceptable. These cats sometimes need to be the only pet in the household, but sometimes, if carefully matched, they can be paired with a more laid-back confident male or female cat.

The Shy Kitty

The shy cat will be nervous and standoffish and sometimes hide when placed in new situations. They feel out the situation before joining in, and might hide for weeks after going home. The shy cat needs time to feel comfortable with any change and the patience of their new people to blossom in their new environment. Sometimes it can be hard to allow them the time they need to feel comfortable, but in the scope of a lifetime in a home it is well worth it. Usually the best placement for the shy cat is to be in a quiet home without kids, loud noise and commotion. They are very likely to develop a special bond with their chosen person.

The Undersocialized

NO I DON'T LIKE THAT BIG TWO-LEGGED ANIMAL. Like the shy cat, the undersocialized cats are nervous around new situations, people and pets. If kittens are not handled by humans within the first three months of their life, they will likely never be comfortable with humans. They tend to be "cat cats," meaning they prefer the company of other cats and not people.

In extreme cases the undersocialized cat is sometimes labeled a "spirit" cat, because they prefer to remain "invisible." They should not be confused with feral cats. There are things to do to make them feel more comfortable and gain their trust. I remove all places where the cat can completely hide. The base of the bed that cats can hide under is removed, radiator bottoms are blocked off as well as underneath desks. Instead I provide a place for the shy or under-socialized cat to hide in plain sight, such as some hidey holes, a blanket-covered cat tree, or cat igloos. I can see them and they can see me. Soft music and a pheromone called Feliway® which comes in a spray or a plug in sometimes helps. Cats react strongly to smell and the pheromone smell says nice calm kitty. Patience, Patience, Patience is key.

Undersocialized cats can successfully be introduced into a home where their guardian understands that they may never be lap cats or be in the middle of things, but will be the cat living on the fringe. They can happily live out a life adoring another feline in the house.

Single Kitten Syndrome

Single Kitten Syndrome kittens are those that are raised without siblings or other kittens. In rescue we try and pair up kittens in a foster home to go home, or send them home with another like-aged cat. That is not always possible. These kittens can be very rough and bite and scratch, because they are never taught by their siblings what is okay and what is not. The job is left to the owner or other pets to teach them not to jump on their backs, try and wrestle every chance they get, attack their humans' hands and legs, and generally annoy the older pets of the household. A loud NO, a spray water bottle, air blowing or whistle goes a long way as well as consistency. They eventually catch on. As with the shy kitty, it takes Patience with a capital P.

Too Many Changes

Too many changes just shut down some of the cats. They seem to be in shock and turn inward. Some just give up and stop eating. Others cats will growl and hiss or become aggressive. These cats are the ones that the shelters can't place and our rescue group is most often called to help with. They are also the ones most likely to be euthanized at the shelter because they are labeled unadoptable. It sometimes takes us multiple trips to the shelter to evaluate these cats to give them a chance to calm down, but sometimes we know they must get out of the shelter environment as quickly as possible or they will die.

Once in rescue, if we can keep them eating and using the litter box, it really is a matter of time before they come around. Sometimes it takes a week, sometimes two weeks, and sometimes longer. Because we don't take aggressive cats into our rescue, it is important to know the difference between an aggressive cat because he or she is mean or "broken" and the one that is on the defensive because they just don't know what to expect next. It can be very difficult to tell the difference. You would not recognize some of these cats once they realize they are safe. The turnaround is stunning.

Lost My Human

So many people don't prepare for the eventuality of their or their loved ones going into a nursing home or dying. What is going to happen to their beloved pet(s)? Yes, you can ask a family member to take them, but most of the time their situation dictates that they can't or they won't when the times comes. Sometimes the cats are younger but much of the time they are older companions with no hope of making the cut of yes or no at the shelters. This is not the shelter's fault. With so many pets needing a space there is no way the shelters can accommodate everyone forever. The cats arrive at the foster homes depressed and grieving. Their person is gone and their life is gone. They give up. As a cat foster parent, we realize that the most important thing is to get the cat to eat and use the litterbox. All the rest takes time and love.

The Overly Needy Cat

"I want to be your shadow!" Siamese cats tend to be very needy to begin with. In their own home, they are ever-present, in your lap, touching your hands while you type on the computer, calling to you if they don't know where you are. They love their person. They want to be with them. Multiply that by ten and you will get a glimpse of the cat that is overly needy. We call it separation anxiety in dogs and it also happens in cats. They can become very vocal or aggressive to stop you from leaving or can stop using the litter box. How to solve it? Good question? The answer is to prove to the cat that you are there for good. That is hard to do in a foster home situation, but once they are home for the long haul this behavior will diminish.

Lost and Found

Why would someone abandon a Siamese Cat? I hear this all the time. Of course, there are lots of reasons. We can't ask the question of the person doing it, but we can come up with lots of reasons, which are all unacceptable. Most of the population don't understand the dangers out in the world. Most cats don't know how to find food, find shelter, escape from predators, deal with nasty humans or other cats who don't want them in their territory. Would you put your child outside and expect them to survive? I can't imagine how frightened a previous house cat feels at being thrown out to forage on its own.

The people who rescue these cats are heroes. We call them Good Samaritans. They step forward when most others will not. Whether they know what to do after they rescue the cat is another story.

These cats are sometimes in tough shape and require vet care, along with testing to make sure they are not already carrying parasites, or diseases such as feline leukemia and feline AIDS, which can be contiguous to other cats in an existing household. Depending on what shape they are in when they come to rescue, most of these cats bounce back. A lot of TLC, good food and a safe place go a long way to get them back to health both physically and behaviorally.

Geezers

Geezers are cats that are older than thirteen years. Siamese cats generally live a long life. Many we know of live into their late teens and early twenties. That means that at thirteen, there may be another seven years of love in their lives. In rescue, it is difficult sometimes to figure out the age of the rescue cats but there are things to look for to give you a clue that they are older. The first thing veterinarians look at are teeth to tell age, but Siamese cats usually have horrible teeth, so it is not that easy. What I look at first is those Geezer Meezer eyes. The oldsters have marbled eyes. Some are receded, depending on health. The next thing to look at is body condition. At a certain age, their rear area starts to lose muscle tone so the back of their body looks a bit sunken in. Sometimes the fur can look like it is a bit sticky. If the cat is not declawed, look at the claws to see how thick they are. Oldsters have thick claws.

That said, in my opinion they are the most loving, funny, amazing cats to have in your home. They are full of personality. There is no hidden agenda. What you see if what you get. There are no guarantees for how much time you have with your beloved companion but every one of these cats give you a massive amount of love and loyalty.

The Only

One of the most difficult cats to place in rescue are the cats that have to be an "only." These cats HATE other cats. They exist to either torment them or hiss and hide from them. It truly limits where we can find homes for these cats. Only cats typically have strong "DIVA" or "KING" personalities and do not want to share their human. They are usually very bonded to their person(s) and will be the BEING in charge of their home. They also tend to be the soul kitties of their forever homes.

Each and every one of these types of cats can vary and have a variety of the behaviors described. That is what makes working with them so interesting. In rescue, we work as guardians to learn about, rehabilitate our rescued cats and to find a responsible loving home for the benefit of all members of the family. After working with so many foster cats I can definitely say that each one has been unique with special qualities. I continue to learn something new with each one.

This book contains stories of cats rescued through Siamese Cat Rescue and some not. They have been contributed by myself and others. We have had the privilege to help these cats move on to their second life.

Andrew, the Lazy Susan Cat

Andrew – Evaluation

*A*ndrew's beloved person passed away, and her daughter Melissa tried to fulfill the promise she made to her mom by taking Andrew into her home. Andrew never trusted strangers and was extremely bonded to his person for all of his ten years. It was not surprising that Andrew did not transition well to this very busy, noisy home with kids and people in and out all the time. Andrew spent most of the next six months hiding in the "lazy Susan" located in an empty in-law apartment in the house. He was grieving, lonely and scared. As much as Melissa wanted to, she just did not have enough  time to work on building Andrew's trust and confidence. This was not the kind of life Melissa wanted for her mom's cherished companion. With a heavy heart, Melissa contacted Siamese Rescue to try and find a new home for Andrew.

I went with another volunteer to meet Andrew. We found Andrew exactly where Melissa told us he would be—inside the lazy Susan cabinet. There sat a very overweight, nervous Siamese blue point boy in an empty apartment. Andrew was not very happy with being dragged out and put on my lap. We softly spoke to Andrew, stroked him and then brushed him. We were told Andrew loved to be brushed, and he certainly did! With a few strokes, he relaxed and settled onto my lap. I could even hear him purr. It was going to take a different environment for this sweet boy to blossom and love again. The paperwork was filled out and submitted, and Andrew was accepted into the Siamese Rescue program.

Within a week Andrew was transported from his home in Connecticut to his foster mom Mary's home in New Hampshire. This was a long trip for a cat that had only left his home a few times. Andrew came out of the carrier nervous but not as scared as his foster mom Mary expected. He proceeded to let her know in his "Meezer" voice that he was not happy with the trip and another change in his life but well, okay, he would like some brushing and lap time.

Andrew – Diary of a cat in foster care
April 13, 2013 - Adopted June 5, 2013 - 11 Years Old

What a yapper! Mostly complaining, I think. I expected a fearful cat and yes, he walked with his belly to the ground but wasn't terribly frightened. Relaxing under a blanket, he let me pick him up, brush him and pet him. I'm was going to have to control his food intake as he was rather chubby. He did seem to be a very nice, although at that moment he was a bit nervous.

Arrival, Day 1

I figured I would mention that an adopter was going to have to have a carrier larger than what Andrew arrived in. It was much too small! I'm not sure how they got him in but I took the top off for him to get out. I kept noticing a slight poop aroma about him but didn't see anything on him nor in the carrier which was lined with a clean towel. When I removed the towel, I discovered old runny poo dried onto the bottom or the carrier (ick factor). I'm talking really old, dried-on, hard to clean up poo! It had been the source of the smell, as now the carrier was cleaned up and in the basement, I could no longer smell it. I can't imagine him having to endure that on his ride up here. But other than that, he had a clean nice coat. It probably had gone unnoticed, as it was in the back of the carrier.

Day 2

He ate some watered-down wet food last night. I watered it down, because I could tell from the smell of his breath his teeth must hurt. I did see him eat some dry kibbles during the evening and he just swallowed it—no chewing, so I thought making his wet food soupy might be easier for him to eat. There was litter box usage overnight. Andrew's former person sent along yesterday newspaper litter and it was hard to tell with that stuff if he peed but I think he did. He is bonding easily to me, but not so much with my husband. I thought he'd be happier with an older female and probably no pets but was not going to limit him to that yet.

Day 3

Andrew ate well overnight (yay). I was feeding him ¼ cup for his dry food (Iams Weight Management) in the morning and again at bedtime. I also gave him ½ can of Fancy Feast mixed with water. Last night he ate all of his wet and most of the dry.

He was quite the talker in the morning. The pile of cat toys I put under the cat tree last night were all over the room this morning.

Day 4

He was eating better. This morning both his measured portions of wet and dry were gone and his water bowl was down by about a third. When I got home from work he'd eaten his morning portion of wet food and the dry was ignored. I would love to see him switch to more wet over dry (which was his only food before). He was using the litter box and all looks normal there, now that he was eating better.

Andrew was getting braver. When I was his room I would leave the door open and while I was logging into the computer he nearly stepped over the threshold into the hallway—but then stopped himself. Then he ran and hid under his blanket. Baby steps for him. When I take him out of hiding, he is very loving and adores his brushing sessions (a definite key to his heart).

Andrew was a nice cat overall, just a bit cautious. My dog was in the room with us earlier too—again, Andrew was cautious but not aggressive and not terrified.

Day 5

Since all systems are go (eating/litter box, etc.) I figured it's time for Andrew to start getting some form of exercise, otherwise he'd lay under his quilt 24/7. I started bringing him into the living room in the evening—he would "yell" at me about it and then scamper back to his room.

Day 7

Andrew's trip to the vet was quite noisy! He had 8 dental extractions (4 lower front, 4 upper back). Poor guy—no wonder he was hiding. His mouth must have felt horrible

Day 16

I think I am finally seeing the real Andrew, and what a bonus.

This evening he (on his own) came into the living room, jumped onto an end table, and announced his arrival. He was stretched out in front of me head-butting my hands so I had to keep back spacing correcting my typing.

Last night I had him on my bed while I was reading and he was in Seventh Heaven! He has the cutest little habit of sticking his tongue out when he's content.

He even greeted my dog this evening with a sniff.

Going Home

It happens all the time, just when our foster cats are ready to go home, they decide to give us the gift of seeing their real personality. Andrew began waiting for me beside the door rather than under his blanket. He was so different than the scared guy who had arrived two weeks before. Maybe his mouth felt better and we all know when we feel good we look good.

If Andrew's previous owner and her daughter could have seen the change in this once cupboard-dwelling Meezer, they wouldn't recognize him.

— *Barbara G., evaluator, Mary P., foster*

Andrews Adopter's Update

Greetings:

Well, the honeymoon is over, and Andrew and I had our first argument. He won.

I usually feed him a bit before we go to bed, and he usually gets up in the middle of the night and I will hear him crunching away. Well, early the other morning, very early, Andrew woke me up by meowing loudly.

I could tell it was a demand, "Get up now and feed me!" Since my alarm is already set to go off at 4:50 am, this was even earlier than that. I just wanted to sleep until the alarm went off, and I told him that I wasn't going to let a Siamese cat tell me what to do. Ha! More loud meowing, which I tried to ignore, so he doesn't think that he is in charge here. The next thing I knew, the light flipped on! That

startled me so much, I did leap out of bed. It seems His Majesty has figured out how to turn the light on, and get me out of bed!

I have attached a picture of Andrew, he looks a little grumpy in the picture, because I woke him this time! Ha! Don't worry, he is such a lovable boy, I could never stay mad at him. He is doing very well with me.

Frankie Blue Eyes

In February of 2015, the Northeast had an "Arctic Vortex" phenomenon. It was so frigid and we had so much snow that animal rescuers stayed awake worrying about what we knew were very dangerous times for abandoned animals living outside. Siamese Rescue was contacted by a "Good Samaritan" living in Fairfield, CT. We all think of Fairfield as being very exclusive and rich. As in all towns, there are very rich areas, but there are also areas on the other end of the spectrum. Frankie's Good Samaritan lived with his mom in a small house built sometime after World War II. Frankie's rescue person was struggling financially just like the rest of the population of the northeast. The recession hit hard for most. He had come home to his childhood home to help care for his aging parents as an adult, and was unable to find employment. Once he found a job, he was working long hours and had an hour commute each way.

One hot summer day he saw a beautiful friendly Siamese cat wandering the neighborhood and wondered what he was doing there. He checked with the neighbors and figured out the Siamese cat did not belong to anyone in the area. He started to feed the cat and named him Frankie Blue Eyes. Frankie was about three years old and had never been neutered. Was he the wandering the neighborhood looking for lady felines? According to the Good Samaritan's mom, he did "travel." I wondered how many gorgeous blue-eyed kittens had been born in the area in that last six months.

Frankie continued to live outside through the summer and fall until the weather became brutally cold. Frankie's rescue person tried to bring him inside but the other cat in residence (another rescued neighborhood stray, also not neutered) would not allow Frankie in the house. I don't know which one of the two was the aggressor, but I do know that having two male un-neutered cats in the house does

6

not work. There was no space for Frankie in the local rescues, but on their list of other rescues to try was Siamese Rescue. It was worth a try for Frankie's rescue person to contact Siamese Rescue.

When I got the email from the director of Siamese Rescue, I immediately contacted the "Good Samaritan," whose name was Scott, to find out more information. It was so cold out that animals

were literally freezing to death and another storm with snow and sub-zero temperatures was expected that weekend. I asked the usual questions. What does the cat look like, when did you first see him, is he friendly, can you handle him, did you check the neighborhood to see if he belonged to anyone? Can you keep him inside? Did you name him? Scott had set up a tarp outside over a picnic table with boxes to keep the cat up off the cold ground but in subzero temperatures it just was not enough.

There was a number of things to work out even before I drove to Fairfield with two other volunteers to hopefully meet Frankie. We already knew we could not leave Frankie in this dangerous situation. We had to have a plan A and a plan B. Plan A was to arrange a visit to a rescue-friendly vet in Fairfield to make sure Frankie was negative to Feline Leukemia and Feline AIDS. I live an hour and a half away and am not familiar with area vets. Scott could not get a vet appointment in such short notice . . . but luck came to call. I had just evaluated another Siamese cat at the home of another rescue person about half an hour away from Fairfield a few weeks before. I gave her a call. She was eager to help and arranged a vet appointment with the rescue-friendly vet she used for her rescue group. They would do the testing and we would wait there for the result. If the tests were negative we could go forward and have the vet update Frankie's vaccines and examine him. If the blood tests were positive he would either be returned to Scott or be euthanized.

A temporary safe home had to be found to keep Frankie for Scott until there was a foster spot for Frankie in Siamese Rescue. Everything was arranged quickly and plans were made to travel to Fairfield on February 10 to meet Frankie and get him out of the icy weather. Would he even be there when we got there? I called Scott and asked him to take him inside or even keep him inside his car for the night. He agreed.

What would we find when we got there? Would this cat be half frozen? What kind of condition would he be in? With the help of the GPS we wound through the neighborhood streets of Fairfield to find the address. When we arrived, I could not park in the driveway because of all the ice and snow. I spotted Scott's car parked in front of the house but did not see Frankie inside. As we walked to the side door of the house Scott greeted us and told us he had taken Frankie inside when he got home from work the evening before. He was inside in a small downstairs bathroom.

The four of us marched into the house, down the stairs into the small area. Stretched out inside a large carrier was a LARGE seal point Siamese cat, with a very round "tom cat" head. Apparently, Scott had fed him very well for the last six months and that probably helped him survive. He looked a bit dirty and worse for wear, but definitely not what I expected to find after this ordeal. Because the bathroom area was so small, we closed the door of the carrier and filed out to drive to the vet's office in a neighboring town with Scott directing us. Plan C was to look Frankie over more carefully and do his evaluation for Siamese Rescue, when we got to the vet's office.

At the vet's office, we gave Frankie to the vet technician to take some blood to do the "SNAP test." The SNAP Combo FeLV Ag/

FIV is a way to quickly detect the presence feline leukemia virus (FeLV) antigen and antibody to feline immunodeficiency virus (FIV). It takes approximately ten minutes for a result. While we waited, the vet examined Frankie. Yes, he was an un-neutered male approximately three to five years old. His paw pads were frostbitten and were peeling off. The vet said they would heal. His ears had deep scrapes on them and were bleeding on the outside. Frankie's fur was coming out where he had gotten clumps of tar around his head, face and neck. We surmised that Frankie had probably gotten up into a car engine or wheel well to stay warm for at least part of the time he was outside. After a ten-minute wait the vet tech announced that his tests were negative/negative and we all could breathe a sigh of relief.

Frankie was a surprising thirteen pounds. He was friendly and allowed the vet and staff to examine and give him his shots, including an antibiotic shot because of the wounds on his ears. I continued to examine him out in the outer office checking his teeth, body, eyes, tail, behavior while his trusted rescue person, Scott, held him. Other clients with dogs and cats wandered in and out of the outer office. None of this fazed Frankie. This amazingly sweet boy was on his way to a safe place and then his future "furever" home. Now we only had get him to his temporary safe home and wait for an open foster space in the New England Siamese Rescue program.

Frankie stayed with his Safe Home rescue people and dog for two weeks. He was not the best house guest because he let his safe home person know he did not want to spend time alone, which is a typical behavior for a Siamese cat. He was not yet neutered and wanted out NOW. He wanted to be with people and apparently, he loved dogs. He demanded that his safe home person sleep with him and would cuddle up with him and his gentle golden retriever dog each night. If he was left alone he would call quite LOUDLY for company. As the saying goes, no good deed goes unpunished.

Safe in foster mom Mary's care
Mary's notes
February 21, 2015

When Frankie first arrived, I was very happy with how well he looked. I really expected worse since this sweet Meezer had been outside during a very cold New England February. He found some safety in a makeshift shelter created by his Good Samaritan. Lucky for Frankie he found the home of someone who cared.

Frankie's first night with me was enjoyable. I woke up during the night to discover Frankie was under the bed covers, down by my feet, with one of my toes wrapped up in his paws. Apparently, his weeks living outside made him really appreciate a warm bed with some warm blankets—and some warm feet!

Frankie came to me as an intact male. I do not understand how people can be willing keep an adult male cat intact! They stink —horribly. Luckily, I had the forethought to schedule Frankie's neuter as soon as I knew he was coming to me and I wouldn't have to deal with the boy stench for very long; although it does take up to two weeks for that smell to dissipate. I anxiously waited for that to happen. Since we do keep new fosters isolated in a room for up to ten days, having to keep the door to his room shut, and it being cold outside . . . oy, the smell.

The honeymoon is over! Although Frankie remained a sweetheart of a Meezer, he wanted back outside. This is quite common with cats that have been outside for a long time. It's the only world they know. Now that Frankie is over his confusion of moving around he wants out, and spent a couple of nights tearing my window blinds apart. Oh well! Won't be the first time I've replaced them for a foster.

Shortly after Frankie's neuter and I was able to determine he was healing nicely, and the possibility of his spraying lessened, I started to let him meet my cats. Frankie loved them! It's great to foster a Meezer who is a cats' cat! Frankie turned out to be nonaggressive toward other cats and enjoyed holding conversations with them.

While Frankie was with me I had an interesting observation—he never went near my doors. He knew they were there but I found it odd than a cat that had been outside stayed away from the doors. He did, however, want to get outside via my windows. I figured I had discovered how this guy came to be outside.

During Frankie's stay with me I had a lab mix dog named Ellie (now at Rainbow Bridge). Ellie was okay with the cats—she couldn't have cared less about them. As long as they didn't bother her, she didn't bother them. Except for Frankie. One evening Ellie was lying at my feet and I could see Frankie watching her. Frankie wandered slowly toward Ellie while she continued to ignore him. I'm sure she was hoping he wouldn't notice her but he did! Frankie decided Ellie was going to be his new girlfriend and mounted her. He even went so far as to grab the back of her neck to hold her down. I so wish I'd been able to get a picture of this. It would definitely have gone viral. But knowing Ellie like I did I figured there'd end up being some fur flying, so I definitely discouraged that move. Silly Meezer!

I have always wanted a male seal point and Frankie was a definite candidate, but I knew he'd also make someone else very happy. My cats are elderly, and having a dog at that time made the timing off. Frankie was a dear, though, and he ended up getting wonderful adopters who also ended up adopting a young female seal point as they knew Frankie would enjoy having a feline friend.

Frankie and his new "girlfriend" had a little adjustment period, but a very short one, and the last update was they get along great! It's what we love to hear.

Frankie went home to his new family March 15th. It could not have been a better fit.

Frankie must have been someone's feline family member at one time as he completely trusted us and showed no signs of being feral. We have no idea how he came to be outside and on his own for the months we know about but somewhere in his life he knew love.

The most intriguing thing about Frankie's personality was his love of dogs. I mean that literally! Although his hormones were settling down, my 60-pound dog found herself becoming the subject of Frankie's "love" on a couple of occasions. I told Frankie just because he sleeps snuggled up to Ellie doesn't mean he can have his way with her.

Frankie was a true "save." Those of us involved with Frankie's rescue are thankful the Good Samaritan looked for Siamese Rescue and contacted us. Frankie had endured enough cold and snow to last him a life time. He now has a safe warm home with plenty of food and his adopters are even considered getting him a dog to call his own!

— *Barbara G., Evaluator; Mary P., foster*

Frankie Update

Frankie has adjusted well and is adored by everyone who meets him. He has put on a few pounds and we are working on that. He loves to be with us and meets us at the door when we return to the house. He lost that full winter coat and is darker now. He is a beauty but does like to give little bites. Anyhow if you can't already tell he is a very important member of the family who is loved!

Annie with the White Sneakers

Sometimes the best-thought-out plans don't seem to work the way you want. I received an email in late June notifying me that there was a Siamese cat that had been hanging around an antique store in Stamford, Connecticut for several weeks. The owner of the store had been feeding her and noticed she seemed to be getting rounder in the middle. A local rescue had been contacted and they contacted Siamese Rescue to see if we could get her into our program.

Thanks to Cora at Pitter Patter Rescue, the Siamese was trapped and brought to the vet, where she delivered five kittens the very next day. The vet verified that the new mom was approximately eight months old. We figured out that this still very young cat had been at least two months out on her own. It was amazing that she had survived. Would she be too wild or undersocialized to save? We would have to wait to find out.

I named her Annie, and we now had to wait for her to wean her kittens before we would know more. Annie was an excellent mamma and loved the kittens.

She would coo, clean and care for them, but remained in the metal cage at Cora's for the next eight to ten weeks. Cora would not dare let her out in the bedroom with the kittens—she was not sure she would be able to get hold of her again. At eight weeks old, three of the kittens died of an unknown virus. The surviving two and Annie remained healthy. Cora told me it

13

happens; it is just the tragedy of rescuing kittens. She reassured me not to worry about Annie's health. Cora has been rescuing kittens for 26 years and I truly trust her opinion.

Annie was spayed (she had already gone back into heat) and Cora let us know it was time to get her out of the cage. Annie was now ten to eleven months old and quite traumatized by her experiences and missing her kittens. Initially I could easily pick her up from the cage at Cora's and hold her. She had no aggression at all. I found a temporary foster home for Annie so she could be outside the cage and in a spare room but because it takes a lot of time and knowledge to work with scared under-socialized cats it did not work out. She was still terrified of humans. Now that she was going to be in open room it was not going to be easy. Annie was accepted into Siamese Rescue and transferred to my foster room. This big scary human lady was going to have to prove herself.

Transforming from a scared, shell-shocked-looking cat who was afraid to move a muscle took time. Annie started to be out in the evenings in my foster room, romping around the room, playing with her toys while I sat on the bed. I got her to play with the mouse on a string and I finally saw some playful kitten behavior. I believed she was still stuck in survival mode. If she was in her safe spot I could easily pet her all over. I don't know how much human interaction she had being out on her own since she was six months old. I spent many evenings playing with her from afar and days sitting on the bed with her in a cat fabric cube in my lap as I pet her. I used kitten purring sounds on YouTube and would play them to Annie, believing it would be a familiar sound that would be soothing to her. She loved the mouse on a wire toy and would eagerly wait for me to play. She progressed to coming closer and closer to the bed where I was sitting. As long as I did not stand up we were good.

After a few weeks Annie progressed to sitting at the door of the foster room (I have a screen door) and she would call for my personal cats. She clearly would have liked to be friends but my three had no interest so I was not able to test it out. I did think she would benefit from being with another cat.

I worked hard to gain her trust and to get her to relax more with humans, and we made strides but there was more work to do. The question was, did I keep her longer and continue work on getting her to come closer and trust me more? If it is the right home, there is some point in cat rescue that you know it is time for your precious fosters to go home.

Annie's approved adopter was aware that she would possibly never completely trust humans. Her previously adopted cat, Frankie Blue Eyes, on the other hand, would be the perfect ambassador and teacher in Annie's fur-ever home.

On October 17, 2015 Annie went home to New Hampshire to her forever family. Reports are that Annie will join Frankie in the living room. They have become good friends and romp around and play. Annie is still not relaxed around her humans but who knows what will come with time, love and patience.

— *Barbara G., foster*

Frankie and Annie in their new home together!

The Neighbors' Cat: Azul
8/20/15

*I*t was a very busy summer with traveling, guests coming to visit from out of town, and of course, Siamese Rescue work. We had a very strange dry spell without request for help rescuing Siamese cats in the spring months, but rescue requests for Siamese cats in New England picked up by the time the month of July peeked out its sweaty face. In came Lily to me to foster; Daisy came to Diana, Oscar and Pashka Jolue came to Diane, Mieka and Mokie came to Trish and then to Peter. Dexter came in and went home to his forever home. Fiona and Jasmine were waiting for their dentals to go home, and Shadow and Ruby were still waiting for their perfect place. All of the foster homes were full here in the northeast and in all of the organization, so when I got a call about a cat needing help on August 20, I clenched my jaw and started the process.

I received a call from my friend Helen, who is the Animal Control Officer in my town. We had worked together in the past and keep running into each other at the rescue vet's office or other town events. Helen is one of those people you instantly like when you meet her and she always goes the extra mile for the animals. Most towns do nothing for cats, since there is no law protecting them. Animal Control is busy enough with all the other emergency calls they get. But this Animal Control Officer is my hero. Helen was calling to tell me that she had taken an eight-year-old neutered male Siamese cat from his deceased owner's home and was holding him at the animal pound. The daughter of the owner had signed the cat over to Animal Control, as she lived in another state and her family was allergic to cats.

The cat, named Azul, was in a cage in the back of the pound listening to barking dogs 24/7. Helen was able to take him out of the cage and keep him in the office when she was there but

16

it was not a great environment for Azul, who she described as a sweetheart. She had all his records, which showed he was up to date on his vaccines and ready to go. All he needed was to test negative to Feline Leukemia and Feline AIDS.

The next morning, I went to meet Azul at the Animal Control office with two other volunteers. We walked to a very small cement building with fenced-in runs with very loud barking dogs jumping in them. I had been in Animal Control facilities before and this was similar but smaller. Helen and ACO met us and let us in the office where Azul was waiting for us under one of the two desks. Azul was an overweight gorgeous lilac point Siamese cat (silver color with gray extremities) and a slightly wedge-shaped face. He greeted us with a gravelly Siamese voice that sounded like someone who had too many cigarettes. At twelve pounds, he was a big boy. After a few minutes of looking at all of us, he decided, "Wow, people to pay attention to me!" and came over to get petted and talked to us. We took pictures and videos, checked Azul over from ears to paws and held him in our arms. At one point he wrapped his long tail around volunteer Peter's legs to let him know not to leave. We were all besotted with Azul. But we did have to leave.

I filled out the paperwork online to get Azul into Siamese Rescue, uploaded the pictures and video and waited to hear if and when Azul would be accepted in the Siamese Cat Rescue program. I knew we had no foster space in Siamese Rescue. That had been a problem all summer. To try and find a place for animals in crisis was tough. But we had done it before. To try and bridge the time gap between getting all the paperwork and other requirements done, we often need to find a temporary safe place or temporary safe home.

When I tell you there are wonderful humans in this world, I truly mean it. Dealing with so many rotten, heartless and uneducated people can make you forget that there are some wonderful angels among us willing to help when asked. I know two such ladies and have called on them to help "safe house" our rescue cats in the past. I tend to do things in the big way. Not loud big, but I try and cover all bases when I ask someone to do something. Any cat we take has to test negative to Feline Leukemia and Feline AIDS and receive at least their Rabies vaccine. If needed, they will get flea treatment as well. So, with no place to put Azul in Siamese Rescue yet, we proceeded to get everything ready for him including a safe home.

Helen met me at the vet's and Azul was "SNAP tested" for Feline Leukemia and Feline AIDS. He was negative so we were ready for the next step. That evening I opened the large folder of papers that Helen had given me to read over and organize them for his new foster home. As I read the name and address of his deceased owner, my mouth fell open. Azul had lived a half a block away from me! In fact, I could gaze out my living room window and see the yellow Colonial he had lived in for two years. The goosebumps ran up and down my arms. I had had no idea.

Azul went to stay with Evelyn, who lives in my town. Evelyn is a long-time rescue friend who has helped house cats "officially" and give them a safe place until we had space in Siamese Rescue. After a short stay with Evelyn, a space opened for Azul and he went to his Siamese Rescue foster home with Trish and Peter. Having never been with other cats that we knew of, Azul did not easily transition to being out and about with Trish and Peter's personal cats. There had been so many changes for this boy. He needed a little time to decompress before he would go home. That was his foster mom's and dad's job until his new person, Rachel, fell in love with him and he was quickly adopted. He is now in his forever home where he is king. He sleeps with his people at night and enjoys his special food and brushing.

Now when I look out my living room window, I glance at the yellow Colonial, which has now been sold to another family, and think how small the world is and how the fates brought me to Azul and Azul to his new fur-ever home.

— Barbara G., evaluator; Trish M. foster

Update: Above is a picture of Azul with his kitten – also rescued by his new person. He is a loving and diligent caregiver to Oscar the kitten.

Siamese Rescue — To the Rescue!
Tori's Tale

The expression "It takes a village" is very apropos for many of our adventures in Siamese Rescue. We sometimes change the cat names as we go from rescue person to rescue person and then the adopter either keeps the name or changes it again. Sasha became Tori and then was given another name when she went home to her fur-ever home. I will call her Tori for my part of this rescue story.

In August of 2014, I was visiting my daughter and family who live in southern California when I received a telephone call from my ex-sister-in-law from Connecticut. It took me a minute to register who it was on the phone because we really don't communicate very much. Cathy was calling on my cell phone to ask me if I can help her neighbor who found a stray Siamese cat in her back yard. She obviously did not know I was not in the area.

Cathy lives in a very nice condo complex near a very busy main road and it seemed pretty plausible that someone had abandoned this cat expecting someone to find her and take care of her. Her neighbor was calling around to see if anyone wanted the cat, who was being kept in a garage and then soft carrier outside, under the neighbor's deck. There was a very bad heat wave with lots of thunderstorms at night for that whole week. The cat was friendly but clearly did not want to stay in the carrier and kept escaping. The area that she was in was near a very large open field that reportedly had fox and coyote sightings, so not a safe place to be, in many ways.

When Tori was found there was a blue collar on her which had the name "Peanut" on it and a phone number. All the people now involved in figuring out what to do with Tori tried to call the number. No luck! I was 3,000 miles away and could not physically help, but frantically tried to figure out who was closer and available to take Tori out of danger's way. Two people came to mind. Sandy, a fellow rescuer who had helped Siamese Rescue before as a temporary safe house was the first person I contacted. The second was Trish and husband Peter, fellow volunteers for Siamese Cat Rescue and friends from Connecticut.

By the time I reached the two of them it was 9:30 at night. There is a three-hour difference in time from California to Connecticut and I did not even think about that until Trish mentioned how late it was to try and do something for Tori. Sandy agreed to take Tori, and Trish and Peter agreed to bring Tori to her in southern Connecticut. The trick was getting Tori to a vet so she could be SNAP tested for Feline AIDS and Feline Leukemia. The SNAP test is a test where a small sample of blood is dropped on a stick (looks like a pregnancy test). You wait to see what color it turns to see if it is negative or positive. Fortunately, Tori's result was negative/negative.

From that moment, Trish and Peter took over. Meanwhile, I kept trying to call the phone number on the collar. Surprise, someone finally picked up. A man answered and when I explained why I was calling he said this was not his phone but his brother's. It had been left in his car. Did he know if his brother had lost his cat? He said maybe and I gave him all the information of who to contact about the cat but of course no one ever did contact us or anyone else involved. No surprise.

While Tori was at Sandy's house, she was not very friendly. She hissed and growled at Sandy and all the other cats in the room with her. Sandy had cared for lots of elderly cats and some Siamese, but was not familiar with this behavior. I told her it had to have something to do with all the changes in her life and the fact that she was probably in heat. Sandy kept Tori in a large cage because she was afraid she could not safely get her into a carrier if she needed to. Eventually Trish and Peter arranged to get Tori into Siamese Rescue and she was transported to her new foster home in New Hampshire.

"Got Yah"
From Trish:

We were at a restaurant eating dinner when we got the call from BJ about Tori. It was about 8:30 p.m. We finished eating quickly, and as we went home, tried to think of how to handle getting a stray Meezer so late at night. Luckily, we had a large metal kitty play pen on the patio, and a screened-in porch which has hardware cloth around the bottom half to prevent wild animals from getting in. (We have had raccoons, bobcats and coyotes in our backyard). I quickly cleaned the kitty playpen, rearranged the porch so the playpen would fit, and Peter helped me get it inside. I found a litter box, food dish and water bowl, got a kitty bed, and got the play pen set up. I wrapped a sheet around three sides.

I called the number Barbara had given me, and got a woman who said her neighbor now had the cat. I got that number, called, and made arrangements to meet her out in front of her condo. Peter and I drove to the complex about ten miles away, which I knew from going to yard sales there, and found the address. The woman was standing out front with Tori in a soft-sided carrier, from which she said the cat would escape. She told me that she'd tried to find the owner without any luck.

We arrived home around 10:30 p.m. on a hot, muggy August Sunday evening—I had an inspiration on the ride to call the petite girl Sasha. (She was later named Tori by Mary P.) We got Sasha placed in the kitty condo, where she immediately ate. I couldn't bring her in the house because she hadn't been tested and we had a foster in the foster room. After a night of restless sleep worrying about her on the back porch, I got her to my vet early Monday morning for testing. Luckily, I've been taking my personal felines to this vet clinic for twenty years, and the staff is used to me asking for help with rescued Siamese. They tested her and gave her rabies and distemper vaccines. We brought her home, and got the information on the safe house with Sandy.

So off we went to Essex, about thirty miles away, and carried Sasha up to the third floor. At that point, I did an evaluation, taking photos of the very sweet tortie point.

I spent considerable time on Craig's List, Petfinder, the lost and found in several area papers, including the *Hartford Courant,* called animal control in three towns, and tried to track the phone number on Tori's collar, all to no avail. (I have a graduate degree in research and am a decent information broker).

Rescue to Foster to Adoption
by Mary

When I agreed to foster Tori, I was expecting a total hellion! Torties have a reputation of being a bit crazed (for lack of a better word) and although I've fostered a few of them over the years, I have found most of them to simply be fun-loving.

From what I was hearing about Tori's tortie-'tude I had some concerns. And of course, I had to bathe this little underweight creature upon arrival. She had a long, five-hour trip from Connecticut to New Hampshire and at some point, she had peed in her carrier and sat in it. She smelled pretty bad!

Her bath was uneventful and I think she was relieved to not stink anymore. Tori was not spayed when found and most likely her attitude was due to her possibly going into her first heat. She was spayed within two days of arriving here, and she was a bit hissy for a few more days, but once she settled down she became quite a character. At first, I thought she was going to have to be an only cat as she showed some aggression to my own cats. I didn't like what I was seeing, but knowing what going into heat can do to a young cat I was willing to wait it out to see if her behavior changed. And I was certainly glad I waited, but I will give my own cats some credit for teaching Tori some manners!

My cats were elders (two at eighteen years of age and one is fourteen years old) and they've seen a lot of foster cats come and go from their home. I can use them as gauges to a strange cat's ability to live with other pets just by their body language, and even though Tori was hissing and charging at them, my cats didn't seem too concerned with her behaviors.

One night Tori jumped onto the bed with me, and two of my cats happened to be sleeping beside me. Upon getting onto the bed Tori would charge them hissing like a little fiend! Both cats simply turned their backs on her and snuggled back into the blankets. Tori was confused: "Hey, you guys, I'm being bad and tough here, you're supposed to run so I can have your warm spots." Once Tori saw my cats were no longer buying into her bluffs, she ended the behavior. This was good, as now I could see Tori could easily live with other cats. My male tabby even started playing with Tori. A cat's version of tag is always fun to watch, especially when they are enjoying themselves. Zeus and Tori would spend a good part of their evenings chasing each other back and forth, and it was good for such a young cat to have an opportunity to bond with another much larger male cat.

Tori was adopted by a family in New Jersey who had adopted a pair of brothers I fostered a few years ago. Since I already knew the personalities of these two male cats I knew Tori would fit in well with them. One of the brothers is quite playful and full of amusing antics while the other was a bit more serious. I knew Tori would win them over and quickly become their little sister.

And she has—she went from a slight little Meezer dumped into a field to a much-loved little sister for two Meezer brothers and a sweet family member for her adopters.

— *Trish M., evaluator; Mary P., foster*

New Beginnings
Momma Penny with Linc and Zelda

*W*hen you hear the word *hoarder*, it conjures up visions of horror. The visions are true. For the cats who are living and trapped in these horrendous situations, they know nothing else but fear, being hungry and struggling to survive. The person who takes in the first un-spayed and un-neutered cats has no idea how things will spiral out of control so quickly with the birth of litter after litter. Kittens are cute and fun to cuddle and play with, until the next set is born. The first group is forgotten, and as they grow up they become more and more undersocialized. They will never be able to feel comfortable interacting with human beings. There is such a small window of time to socialize kittens. It really is before twelve weeks of age.

A fellow volunteer, Peter, got the call and asked me to go with him to the house thought to have fifteen cats. We were to try and place a few of the Siamese-cross cats in our breed rescue organization. The total turned out to be more like *thirty-five* cats, plus newborn kittens and pregnant cats. In these groups were cats from litters now one year old, six months old, five weeks old, and, as we discovered when we arrived, two-week-old kittens living in a dresser in the basement of the house.

As we entered the house, the smell hit us like a wall. It went up our noses, into our hair and clothes. The smell was a mixture of un-neutered males, spraying cats, and urine. I suspect it was toxic to the lady and her son who lived there, and also to the cats. We were introduced to the upstairs cats. Each one had a name. These were cats that had had more socialization but still bolted when they saw strangers. The cats sat on every chair and behind what little furniture that was there. In this group were a number of black cats and Siamese crosses.

As we progressed in the house, we were taken into the owner's bedroom where three five-week-old Siamese-cross kittens were being kept. The momma cat, named Honey, was also kept in the room to make sure they would be nursed. Honey was part of a previous litter under a year old that had been born in the home and not totally socialized. The owner promised to keep the mamma cat in the room with the kittens to feed them until we could arrange to get them all into a safe home and then into Siamese Rescue.

Our next area to investigate was the basement. Most of the cats were down in this area, hiding in the rafters, behind a wall of plastic boxes, and sitting on whatever was available. One very large litter box sat in the middle of the room, with urine stains spreading out around the basement cement floor. There was an old white Formica® dresser. When I looked in one of the drawers there were two tiny kittens in it. I quickly closed the drawer so I did not spook the kitten's mother. The owner figured out that Penny must be the mom of the kittens and had hidden them in the drawer. But Penny was nowhere to be found. The kittens were about two weeks old but the owner had no idea they were there.

While we could not take the non-Siamese cats, our volunteer Peter did manage to find other rescue groups to rescue over twenty-five of the cats. No cat had been spayed or neutered, and not one had seen a vet. To be able to go into that hell and come out the other side saving so many lives was a challenge.

Approximately a week went by and we went back to check up on all the kittens. We had arranged for Honey and her three now-six-week-old kittens to be taken to a safe house and began the paperwork to get them accepted into the Siamese Rescue program. The mamma cat, Honey, was too "mixey" for our program. She had a lot of white on her body and most people coming to Siamese Cat Rescue to adopt a cat would not recognize her as a Siamese Cat. We found a temporary foster home for her and she was eventually adopted by a local family.

Two of the kittens came to me to foster and the third went to another foster. That is a story told in my first book. This story is of the two younger kittens with mom Penny. By the time we went back to check on the kittens, the kittens had been moved to another area of the basement and had crept under a wooden pallet with plastic storage boxes stacked on top of it. It was dangerous for such small kittens to be lying on the cold cement floor. We moved the

plastic storage boxes and the wooden pallet to get to the kittens and transferred them up to the owner's bedroom with their mom, Penny, who was not too happy about these humans and their interference.

After arranging a safe place for the kittens and their mom we went back to rescue Penny and her kittens. She tolerated our presence and the kittens but Penny was barely out of kittenhood herself and we were concerned she would not take care of the kittens. In reality it was too late to change Penny's behavior but we could work on making it less traumatic to be with humans. Penny was what we call a "cat's cat"—she preferred to be with other cats and would truly only relax in their company. Penny stayed in the temporary safe home with her kittens until they were weaned. The kittens blossomed in the care of their safe home foster. They received the socialization that their mom did not and were a delight to watch.

*Linc and
Zelda with
Momma Penny*

Penny eventually came to me as my foster. She was sweet and absolutely had no aggression. In the weeks that followed Penny spent most of her time in a fabric cube or under the bed. I would take her out and cuddle her under a blanket by my side or on my lap a few times a day. Eventually I let my personal boy cat, Dunkin, in the room. A-ha, that got her interest. Dunkin was playing with a feather toy on the other part of the bed. Penny stretched, walked over to him, tried to bump heads . . . and then, because Dunkin was not interested, jumped off the bed, went to the scratching post, stretched a little and laid down next to it. She did not go back in her cube. I had found the answer. Penny had to go to a home with another cat that she could be best friends with. The family had to know that she probably would never be a lap cat or even care about the humans in the house.

Yes, we did find a wonderful home for Penny, or Penny Lane as she was dubbed by her adopters. They adored her. She fell in love immediately with their other cat Norman. Apparently, she made him a little crazy trying to be by his side all the time. Life was good for the next couple of years. Unfortunately, Penny escaped the house and went missing. There is no chance that she will be caught by conventional means. There have been sightings by neighbors,

Linc, Gizmo and Zelda

but this was a heavily wooded area with lots of wildlife. There are also two local barns where Penny has been seen with some other strays being fed there.

Penny's kittens were named Zelda and Linc by their new family and live in Northern Connecticut with their human family and their adopted brother Gizmo. When I look at their first pictures and the updated pictures from their new home, I am just amazed that these tiny babies are all grown up happy and well adjusted.

— *Barbara G., evaluator and foster*

*I*magine being alone, hungry, cold and wet in a burned-out former industrial building. Imagine having to suffer this fate after having once been a beloved feline friend to someone. Imagine not knowing what happened to the person who once offered love, a full belly and warmth. Imagine wanting to return to that life but not finding anyone who cared enough to save you. Imagine the happiness when a caring Animal Control Officer found you and knew you needed help, and took you in.

Then Siamese Rescue came to your aid with a caring and nurturing foster home where once again you were warm and dry; fed and loved; able to sleep in a soft bed and purr from happiness and contentment rather than the purrs that sometimes signal dying.

You were named after the building where you took refuge since no one knew anything about your past.

You were brought back to health and a normal body weight by your Siamese Rescue foster who was terrified she'd lose you. You came to her weighing only 3½ pounds but she was able to get you back to a healthy weight of 6 pounds.

You were very sick when you arrived at your Siamese Rescue foster home but your caregiver fed you good food, made sure you had the vet care you needed, and very importantly showed you love again.

Your Siamese Rescue caregiver loved you so much she let you stay with her.

You are, once again, a much-loved feline friend for someone.

If your Siamese Rescue caregiver had not adopted you she would have made sure you went to a home that would make sure you were safe, warm, fed, and loved for the remainder of your days. In spite of the rough time you had living in that burned-out former industrial building Siamese Rescue was waiting to take you in and help you become the loved Meezer you once were.

— Story by Mary P.
Trish M., evaluator, Paula S., foster

My Story
by Little Miss Whitney Pratt

I refuse to say how I got my many scars, but I can tell you I had a hard life when I lived in Wallingford, Connecticut. I ran away from home in search a new home worthy of me. I walked and looked, and looked and walked, but didn't have any luck finding my new home. I finally found an empty factory building owned by Pratt & Whitney and settled in.

Much to my annoyance there were no food servants and I had to eat whatever I found, and I kept getting skinnier and skinnier. Then winter came, and it got cold! I lived there for a long time.

Then, much to my amazement, some old wood caught fire and then there were sirens and men in yellow overalls who sprayed water everywhere. Once the commotion was over, I marched up to the fire chief and screamed at him. I NEED a food servant! And I needed one NOWWWWW. He listened to me and called David from Animal Control.

David came right over, took one look at my skinny self, and decided that I needed to get to the hospital fast. The doctor was very worried about me and thought I might not make it through the night, but I was the happiest I had been in a long time. By morning he decided that I hadn't used up all of my nine lives, so David came and took me back to the shelter and he named me "Pratt Cat." But then he did the very best thing he could for me…he called Siamese Rescue, that's when things started happening fast.

Siamese Rescue has many very dedicated volunteers. Mary, the New England coordinator, put the wheels in motion. She asked Trish, a volunteer who lived closest to the Animal Shelter, to evaluate Pratt Cat as soon as possible, and she asked Paula if she would foster her if she was accepted into the program. Trish determined that Pratt Cat was a good candidate for Siamese Rescue, Mary agreed, and so did Siri. The very next day Trish was picking her up for transport to Paula's for fostering.

So, then this nice lady and her husband came to the shelter to get me! Yippee! I'm outta the shelter and going home! It was warm in the car and Trish kept talking to me and telling me I was one lucky cat. And I was thinking I liked this new mom. Then we were in a parking lot and all of a sudden, this other lady was there and I got moved from one carrier into another. This wasn't what I thought home would be like. That lady talked to me too, and she too said I was one lucky cat. Maybe that's my new name—Lucky Cat's a better name than Pratt Cat!

Then we got to a new place. The lady said I was home. As I was whisked through the house I sniffed the air and knew that other kitties lived there, and this great big nose sniffed me too. I was glad to be safe in a carrier. Then the lady said, "Here's your room," with food and water and a heated bed. But I still thought the carrier was the safest place to be and hunkered down in the back. She didn't like that idea and pulled me out and got me all snuggled under a fuzzy blanket where it was warm. I hadn't felt this warm in weeks.

She said Pratt Cat was a silly name for such a sweet girl. She tried several names out on me, I refused to react to any of them. Then she said that I would be Whitney Pratt.

All I wanted to do was to stay in that warm bed. But the lady insisted that I needed to eat. I didn't tell her, but I really was too sick and weak to eat. Somehow, she knew that anyway. She would mix up a batch of yummy liquid goop and then she'd squirt a little bit into my mouth. It tasted good, and I really liked the attention. She did that many times a day for many days. Tee hee, I liked the attention so much that I tried to convince her that I was still too weak to eat on my own. I was sneaking food out of the dish when she wasn't looking, but somehow, she knew anyway.

All during this time she kept putting her fingers around my middle to feel how skinny I was—she said she could touch her fingers through my belly. She counted my protruding ribs too. I put up with that indignity because I was home. Then one day she told me she was my foster mom, and that now that I was getting better she would work to find me the perfect home. Shoot, I thought this was my home.

I'm little and have pearly white teeth and perfect gums too so everybody thought I was a young girl. When I finally got strong enough, foster mom scheduled me for a spay and my vaccinations. The doctor shaved my belly to look for a spay scar and didn't find one—he didn't ask me first. So, in I went to the surgery room. HA! I fooled him. I was spayed already, but that doctor used an incision on my side. Then the next morning when foster mom came to get me, the doctor told her he hadn't seen a vet use that method in decades. Then he said that I was an old cat who once had been fat. How dare he say that! Then he said that since he had me open he rooted around to look at my innards. He said I was old! At least twelve, if not older. And that I had the fat deposits of a fat cat! Then foster mom said she had thought I was about twelve, too, because of the beautiful blue facets of my eyes. So much for trying to keep that stuff secret. Harrumph. I screamed that I wanted out of there. If she's going to call me Whitney, I'm going to use my lungs!

A few days later, I was in foster mom's lap staring at her with my beautiful blue faceted and sparkling eyes sending her messages. I sent her a vision of my living here forever and her being my mom. Day after day I stared and stared trying get that message through to her. I can look pretty adoring when I want something. And I really wanted this to be my new home. She finally heard me! But she had conditions. I would have to leave this warm room so other kitties could be rescued, and I'd have to move downstairs. She said I would have to get along with an old guy named Rudy, and a diva named Petey and a big dog named Mona. I already knew about them, and had seen that dog's big nose. I quickly agreed!

I was home! I was home! I was home!

I've been here almost two years now. Last year, both Rudy and Petey went over the Rainbow Bridge, and Mom adopted a little guy from Siamese Rescue who was found in a feral colony in

Richmond. Mom calls him Tony. I call him "the pest." But I do like to play with him; we run around the house together, and box under the doors. I even like Mona too, all 80 pounds of her. She gives me big wet kisses.

I've been training Mom to give me kisses too. For weeks and weeks, I would sit in her lap after breakfast, I would sit up very straight and tall, then I would push my head up as high as I could. Finally, I got through to her, and she kissed the top of my head. We do that many times a day now. She says it might be too many times, but I disagree, there's no such thing as too many kisses. I'm so happy, and I want Mom to know how much I love her, so after she's asleep I return the kisses by giving the tip of her nose a little lick or two in the middle of the night. I'm so happy.

Thank you, Siamese Rescue, you've made Little Miss Whitney Pratt very warm and happy.

Spike's Journey

Sometimes you have to wonder why so many bad things happen to one family. I am talking about life changing, heartbreaking things for people and their animals. Spike originally came to Siamese Cat Rescue from the Fairfax Country Animal Shelter in Virginia. He had been well loved by his family, but one of the daughters in the family was allergic to Spike and the doctor recommended that Spike be rehomed. He was given up to a kill shelter and Spike really did not do well there. He had a strong Siamese personality. You know the type: opinionated, demanding, and annoyed when things aren't going his way. Spike was angry, loud, and complaining at the shelter and completely stressed out by the whole experience. This behavior was not surprising in a noisy, smelly, loud, scary, caged environment. It can be terrifying for cats who have never experienced it. In a nutshell, Spike was not going to be adopted at the shelter and he needed to get out of there. Siamese Cat Rescue stepped in and Spike was brought to the Rescue Center in Locust Dale, Virginia.

Spike arrived at Siamese Cat Rescue Center and it did not take long for him to exhibit his strong personality. I believe the term is "alpha cat." He was outgoing, busy, demanding, opinionated, interactive, and curious. Spike does not like other cats, as evidenced by his hissing at any cat that got near him. But he clearly liked people. He did okay with a carefully chosen cat of similar personality but he really preferred humans.

After four months Spike was adopted by an older couple from North Carolina and became strongly bonded to the man of the household. After the couple's grandson was killed tragically in December 2012 at Sandy Hook, Connecticut, they moved to New Hampshire to live near their daughter. In May of 2014 Spike's preferred person, the husband, passed away suddenly. Spike became angry and mourned the loss of his person. He acted out by biting the lady of the house a number of times. It was clear Spike was coming back to Siamese Rescue after eight years: the safety net we promise all our rescued cats was still there. We would find him the perfect fur-ever home.

Back in Rescue
February 2015

Eight years is a long time and the loss of his person was deep. Spike came back to Siamese Rescue angry. His new cat foster dad, Peter, knew all the traits of an angry alpha cat. We have seen it before. It takes time for rescue cats to get over their losses. Spike was no different. He looked almost shell-shocked when I met him at Peter's house when he first arrived. Foster dad Peter felt that this almost-nine-year-old cat had a better chance to find a home if he could be placed with other cats. He would bring Spike upstairs to this family room to familiarize him with the house cats. One of Peter's personal cats, Tony, is a wonderful ambassador cat. He is always ready to go in the foster room and tell the new resident hello. Spike did benefit from Tony's easy-going personality, and after 111 days in rescue, he would play and spend time with Tony but it was never an easy relaxed relationship.

Spike seemed to get along with three of Peter's personal cats, with one exception. He hated Shadow, who was a gorgeous green-eyed black longhair domestic boy. I always wonder if Siamese cats are just plain stuck up! Do they prefer their own kind? I have heard many stories to support this but just as many that did not. The idea was to try and place Spike in a family without other cats.

After almost three and a half months, Spike's foster dad Peter found out that he needed serious heart surgery so Spike was due for another change. He would be moved to my foster room. Would he regress or continue being a now really sweet sometimes persnickety Meezer?

May 2015 – Another page to another story!

Spike arrived at my foster home and inspected the room, used the litter box, had a snack and took a nap in the round comfy Millie bed purring away. I expected some backsliding, with another change in Spike's life but I was pleasantly surprised at how well he did. He loved to sit and sun in the windows and would come cuddle with me. I decided to forgo any introduction to my cats and let him be what he really wanted to be...King Spike of his castle.

His alpha cat reaction had receded a bit with the removal of most the stress in his life. He would play with toys, and especially liked the round scratching post with a ball in it and the feather on the pole. He did like to cuddle with me at night and then retreat to the end of the bed for a while and then go to his window bed.

Spike gave small love nips but did not bite down. I believe if pushed he might go back to the alpha male behavior and could get quite agitated. I would liken it to a child having a temper tantrum, but he was quite sweet and loving to me. He loved his treats and would go to a certain spot to receive them. He liked routine.

Going Home

After two and a half weeks with me, the perfect adopter found Spike. My personal vet office put me in contact with one of their clients named Peter. Yes, another Peter. This Peter was looking for his new fur family member. This time had to be forever. The term it was meant to be fit perfectly. After some back and forth with the vet practice, the prospective adopter got in touch with me. I spend a lot of time letting Peter know "the good, the bad and the ugly" so he was aware of everything and could make an informed decision.

When Peter A. came to meet Spike, it was love at first sight. The fact that Spike would have his person all to himself just felt right. Spike would continue to be mouthy (bite) but not mean or angry... almost like a love bite...a reminder that HE was in charge. Peter would have to remind him NO, no bite, and withdraw.

Spike's person Peter keeps in touch and things are going great. Spike's name has been changed to Bjorn—a more fitting name for such a regal Siamese.

There has been a line of rescue people who have been on board to help this sometimes-crabby character love life again. He will always be Spike to me and I feel so good about the job all the volunteers have done to get him to his new life. If you see his picture these days you will see a relaxed "mush" of a cat with a look of pure contentment, and yes, I am proud to have had a hand in that.

— *Peter K. and Barbara G, fosters*

Taking a Chance on Lucy

*L*ucy lived with the same family for her first seven years. She was probably the beloved baby of the family most of those years until the human babies came into the family. This very modern-style Siamese petite seal point girl had the most amazing personality. To love a Siamese, you need to love the in-your-face personality that most of them have. Lucy was to the extreme. From the minute I saw her picture, which had been forwarded to me from a rescue friend, I was in love. She became my foster and attached herself to my heart.

Lucy had been posted on Craigslist as free to good home. The majority of 20-30-somethings do not realize how dangerous posting their pets to Craigslist is for their beloved pet. As rescue people, we try and educate people. Do you know who is looking at Craigslist to adopt a pet? They are not necessarily the sweet nice family person who loves animals. They can be animal abusers, animal re-

sellers to medical labs or puppy/cat mills . . . or worse. Those horror stories come up again and again about an owner being fooled into thinking their animal will go to a wonderful home just to find out some horrible unthinkable things happen to them. I rarely look at the site for "pets free to good home" but other rescue people check them all the time and forward them to me.

Lucy was being given up because she had been peeing on her owner's bed repeatedly and they could just not get her to stop. She had been treated for multiple urinary tract infections, which had been resolved and still there was a problem. The family vet assumed it was a behavioral issue. The family also thought it was a jealousy thing, because the children, now toddlers, were coming into the parent's bed to sleep, which had previously been Lucy's spot. Something about this description bothered me as well, as the pictures showed this very tolerant Siamese cat being manhandled by a young toddler and seemingly fine with it. I knew I was taking a chance of getting a cat who had behavioral problems peeing outside the box. I suspected there was much more to it. I arranged to get Lucy from a rescue lady I had known for a long time. And she came to me as my temporary foster and then permanent foster for Siamese Rescue.

Lucy was the modern or extreme style Siamese cat. She had a long face, big ears, tubular body and whippy tail. She looked like a show cat. Along with the looks she had the personality of a typical needy, in-your-face, involved Siamese.

I suspected there was something physical going on with Lucy because of the frequency of her using the litterbox. She was very thin with her rear tailbone visible. She could stand to put on some weight, but I did not know what was normal for her. With permission from Siamese Rescue I arranged a vet visit to check and see if there was still an unresolved urinary infection resulting in her having the use the box continually. Because the vet had such a hard time getting a urine sample, she had to stay the entire day. When the tests came back it was found that Lucy did not have a urinary tract infection but did have a lot of blood and white blood cells in her urine. Could it be due to stress? A course of anti-inflammatory medication was started and we would wait to see if there was improvement. We also started special prescription food which was easier on the bladder.

With little or no improvement, there was clearly something wrong which had to be figured out further.

Because Lucy had a difficult time with Clavamox drops (they made her throw up), the vet gave Lucy a Convenia injection, which needed to be repeated in two weeks and the vet would recheck the urine. The vet also suggested giving her ¼ tsp. Miralax in her food once daily and Omega 3/Omega 6 Fatty Acid Supplement, also in her food. She discontinued the Metacam (anti-inflammatory medication) and continued the prescription food tha Lucy had been eating for the last two weeks. The vet suggested that Lucy be on the Convenia (antibiotics) for at least a month before going home.

After a few weeks, Lucy had another vet visit. There had not been much progress with the frequency of her visits to the litter box and she had had one accident outside the box. The vet gave Lucy a second long-acting antibiotic shot and attempted to get an X-ray to see if there were any suspected kidney stones in her bladder causing the problem. The ultrasound showed a shadow but the X-ray could not tell us for sure. A few days later Lucy had surgery, resulting in removal of five kidney stones. The stones were examined to see what they are made up of to see what how to proceed with her care

Lucy did really well after her surgery. She had no problem getting around the room and became quite vocal, wanting food and attention. Her visits to the box became more normal. She was licking the incision but it was not inflamed so I let her be and did not put on the dreaded E-collar (aka "Collar of Shame"). Now I had to fatten her up. She was still quite thin and was always hungry.

Lucy's lucky adopter, Jennifer, waited patiently for Lucy to recover and go home. As it turns out, Lucy loved to drink milk. I could never get her to drink much water. Her new person discovered that Lucy liked to drink milk from her cup. Did she drink milk from her former home's toddler's glass? It was discussed with Jennifer's vet because by now we knew that the bladder stones were calcium, so no more milk. Jennifer solved the problem by giving Lucy water with a drop of milk in it. It was just enough to entice Lucy to drink.

I get regular updates and pictures of Lucy with her new brother Hemi. They look and act like they have been together all their lives and are a source of delight for their person. I am so glad I took a chance on Lucy.

— *Barbara G., evaluator and foster*

*Lucy
and Hemi*

Empty Hallways

It is nigh 2 a.m. ...
do you know where your Geezer is?

I, the Mom Pat, lie in bed reading. It is way late as usual. Next year, the Millennium, I will reset my internal clock from "Night Owl" mode to jive with the rest of the World, I PROMISE. Well, maybe.

Gracie on my chest, eager for her due quality time. A most well-read Meezer, she. I have learned to read between her ears— "her lines"—by holding my book up a bit until my arms quiver. She purrs and licks the hand not petting her. The numbness in my arms is all worth it.

I am suddenly aware of the silence, the absence in the house... "Where is Mork?" The unconscious, instinctive neurons fire in my brain as a knot forms instantaneously in my stomach.

It has been quiet too long, no pacing and YEOWLING at the bedroom door. "Come to bed, TomCat," the Geezer Mork usually howls come the ten o'clock hour, "Airlift me up to the bed with you, let me warm my Geezer chilled paws on yer belly and tuck my head under yer chin and breathe the fluff-a-huffa sleep breath of the ages, NOW-YEOWL!!"

It has been quiet too long. The familiar, perpetual worry is back. Is he sleeping under the lamp in the family room? His 200-watt Reader Light, his favorite spot, under which he fries his brains, was extinguished hours ago, much to his dismay. Or, is he visiting with his sister Mindy (gone from our realm over three years now) on the spot in the darkened living room where she left us? He is surely not in the basement, for his legs will not take him down the stairs any more with bladder intact. He is a proud, clean Geezer and will not withstand that indignity again—the puddle under his paws—better to stay upstairs, and better to pee in the litter box in the kitchen like a WeeMeeze. The KitKat, George (aka Felix, The Wuss, Unger) will lurk around the corner and obsessively cover his droppings, bless his heart.

It has been quiet too long! So where could he be? I worry-wart forward-think to a time when the hallway outside our bedroom door will be dark and silent always of his presence, his asymmetrical gimp, the licking of his chops after a snack, a glimpse of his almost white chest peeking through the dark hallway tunnel, the dull glimmer of once bright crystal blue eyes, the sealy ear points as he slowly approaches and circles the bed like a shark...I do not see or hear these signs of Mork in our hallway...a twenty-something Geezer Meezer cannot last forever. When in doubt, WORRY!

I resist the urge to jump from bed to search for Mork to bring him into our warm fold. It would disturb Gracie's quality time, alone with me, while her brother, George, practices his Mini Howls and Nocturnal Ablutions the basement, the practicing student of Mork. My breathing becomes labored; I take a drag from the inhaler, read and reread the same line fifteen times, eyes darting down the Ranch-O-Rama Bowling Alley hallway of this home of ours, never without Mork.

AAAHHHH!! I hear him! A *click,* his nail along the hardwood floorboards...now his white chest comes into focus and soon the unmistakable YYYYEEEEOOOWWWLLLLL of a chilled, angry Geezer Meezer. I can breathe again, my jaw relaxes. Mork approaches, his shoulders still retain the swagger of his mighty youth, though his sealy tail, once always at high noon, now sags at half mast. His hips, they fail him, too, as he begs, er, *demands* his bed space. "LIFT ME UP NOW-YEOWL!"

Lights out. Another night. Just the five of us, cozy, in bed. The darkened hallway looks different, less menacing now. Mork's evening processional has left a glow of hope. I am thankful for his spunky persistence and his Spirit that keeps him with us these twenty-something years.

Nighty Night to all Geezer MomzNPops who worry about empty hallways and "things that *don't* go bump in the night."

Say Goodnight, Gracie. Say Goodnight, George. Goodnight, Sweet Old Mork.

George and Grace by Mom Pat

Pi, AKA Moon Pie
Rescued October 2, 2012
In Siamese Rescue October 25-December 3, 2012

*H*ow these cats find their way to the feral colony feeding stations we will never know. The feeders are familiar with the cats in the colony and when a new one joins they are observed to see if they are friendly. Pi was being fed at a feral colony station in Worcester, Massachusetts, for over a month before the feeder could get close enough to get a good look at him. The feeder noticed that he had a harness on that was very tight. Pi was caught and another rescue group was called to help.

When the new rescue lady came to see him, she could smell him from the next room. The harness was completely embedded and infected. The vet said he had been living that way for at least a year. It was a kitten-size harness, and as he continued to grow the harness grew into his flesh. The rescue person could not imagine the pain this cat endured.

Pi was rushed to a vet to have the harness surgically removed, given vaccines and neutered. The rescue lady didn't really know what to expect after his surgery. She didn't even know if he was friendly or feral since nobody had been able to touch him. When Pi awoke from this grueling but lifesaving surgery, he slowly head-butted the hand of the vet tech. In spite of his pain and discomfort, Pi quickly relaxed and enjoyed the care and love he got from the vet staff and his rescue people.

After three surgeries to completely remove and repair the damaged tissue, Pi continued to patiently wear his E-collar to prevent him from licking the healing areas. He turned out to be a loving and sweet-natured cat. He was at the vet clinic for several weeks and would ride around the shoulders of the techs. Even when he needed a second surgery to close up the wounds in his armpits, he came through it like a champ. More than forty people came together to donate the $1,000 it took to get him better.

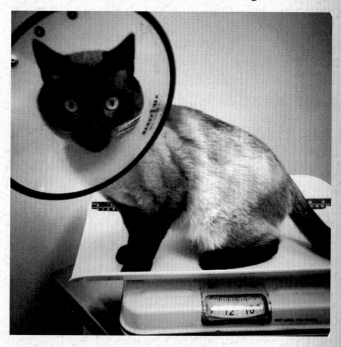

Pi was accepted into the Siamese Rescue program and was then released to the care of a wonderful foster dad who tended to all of his daily medical needs and gave him an abundance of love which Pi returned by purring, kneading and enjoying lap time. This cat was patient and loving and so thankful for the help given him. By November his stitches where ready to be removed and he was ready for his forever home.

At the beginning of December Pi was adopted by another Siamese rescue volunteer who fell in love with him. He went home to spend his first holiday warm inside with the love of a family.

Pi's family now includes two other Siamese Cat Rescue cats and four busy kids. Pi has been re-named Moon Pie and has adorned a few of our Siamese Cat Rescue yearly calendar. He is quite photogenic.

— *D. Hastings, Evaluator; Peter K. foster*

Yule

*Y*ule was adopted in December of 2013 along with another kitten. She was a little on the shy side when adopted, but from the notes I read from Siamese Cat Rescue, all was normal. The family she was adopted into was a mom with three boys, the youngest now five years old and, I was told, was a handful. The other kitten was a flame point and not as shy as Yule and was preferred by the older boys. The mom, now divorced, had moved three times and the home appeared to be chaotic; both the cats were stressed and skittish. Yule developed crystals in her urine which was discovered when she started to pee all over the house. It was mostly resolved by medication but the household environment apparently made it difficult for her to overcome the problem. She did not urinate outside the box in my foster home or at her previous foster home, so I would say it was stress related.

Is she a "project cat"? We were not sure that with time and patience she would settle in and not show the fear she first did. She hid under the bed for the entire month at foster Bonnie's home. Because I have had a lot of experience and success with shy kitties, I took Yule to my foster room to work with her. My foster room does have a bed but it is down on the floor and I have multiple hidey holes (cat igloo type beds) around the room.

Yule as a kitten

Yule loved to be loved while she was inside her cat cave and would headbutt my hands, and was constantly seeking out body massages. She would rest her face on my hands and will roll on her back for belly rubs. After just one week she was half out of her cave enjoying interaction from me but still rushed back to her cave when she got spooked. She had lived with another cat but I suspected she could be a victim cat if chased.

Yule's habits were great. Litter box and eating were fine but she could be a bit picky. I gave her salmon paté soft food and a handful of hard kibble. After the first couple of days of not eating much she did just fine.

We made good progress with Yule in a relatively short time and it was time to find her a forever home and person. I knew it would take a little patience and love but she would blossom into a loving soul kitty who would enjoy the attention and adoration of her person. As it turned out, Yule's person lives in a retirement community and she gives Yule all the attention she needs. Yule still hides when someone new comes, but that is okay with her person. It took some figuring out, but Yule was finally in the right home.

— *Bonnie C. and Barbara G., fosters*

Lily
August 2015

*L*ily looked mostly like a seal point but had a sprinkling of "sugar" on her face and legs. Sugar is the right word, because she was just the sweetest petite girl with a gentle soul and a little voice.

Her previous owner was a young woman who could not afford to keep her and contacted the Animal Control Officer in her town to take her. The first time she could not give her up. The second time she contacted the ACO was a year later and she was ready to give Lily up. Lily had not received any vet care since she was a tiny kitten but nevertheless she was extremely healthy. Obviously, she was well loved because her personality showed she was loving and friendly. Lily had to get used to a lot of change being brought from place to place when her owner moved around, but did just fine.

Lily's person arrived late at our appointed meeting spot. As her person opened the back of a SUV, I lunged to grab Lily, because she had started to run for the woods that surrounded the parking lot. Lily had been loose in the back of the SUV with no carrier to make the transfer safely. Luckily, I had brought one with me to put her in. I carefully bit my lip so as not to give the owner a hard time—I was just happy that Lily was safe in my carrier in my car and headed for a better life.

At first Lily was very sweet, but nervous and a little standoffish. She would spend time under the bed but came out to eat or use the box, and came over to give me a headbutt on my hands. The previous owner said she liked to knead and suckle on her ear. (She was probably taken from mom a little too soon.) After Lily received her rabies vaccine and a flea treatment and deemed healthy by the vet, she needed to be spayed before she could go home.

After a short time, Lily was making good progress with her true personality emerging. She was coming out and spending more time up on the cat tree, on the bed with me and playing with the mouse on the string. She was very sweet but still a little nervous when I did something she did not like. Back under the bed she would go. All I had to do was put her medication in her food and she would eat it. She definitely was food driven.

I had to wait a few weeks for Lily's appointment to get her spay. She spent the night there and came home and ate a half can of food, and meowed for attention. The clinic observed a small umbilical hernia but said it was only cosmetic and nothing neededto be done about it. It really did not take long but Lily was ready to go home.

Carol was to be Lily's new person and was delighted to come pick up Lily at my home. It was love at first sight. I understand it was not love at first sight with her other two cats, as Lily developed a stronger TORTITUDE attitude with Carol's two cats. Eventually everyone has settled in with Lily running the show. Apparently, Lily still loves her food a little too much.

— *Barbara G., evaluator and foster*

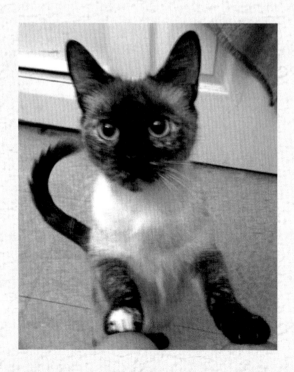

Wren and Whitaker

*I*have never been to Tennessee. I am a homebody in my heart and not the least bit adventurous. That makes it kind of weird that I am involved with cat rescue. My friends and acquaintances from over the years span the United States, Europe, and Australia, but here I sit in a suburb in the middle of Connecticut, happy to be home with my husband and three fur kids.

What was it like to be dumped off in a feral colony in rural Tennessee for Wren? She was most probably still a kitten herself and was found with her own four-month-old black boy kitten (later named Whitaker). There are so many questions. Why was she abandoned? Was she pregnant when she was abandoned or did she already have her baby with her? And why did she only have a stub of a tail? I have asked her rescuers but never got any answers. I doubt if they ever knew.

What I know of Wren and Whitaker's journey starts with a long-time rescue friend from Connecticut and her friend who lives in Tennessee. There are angels in this world who choose to work their magic in different ways. It does not make their life easy or even uplifting. Working with these angels is a privilege. But when you are asked to help, it is never easy.

Planning was a big deal. Wren and Whitaker were coming from a shelter in Tennessee with eight other young kittens. They all had different stories but all were to perish if they stayed in the overcrowded, underfunded shelter. The staff at these shelters work diligently to try to find solutions to get the animals out before they are euthanized. There are now many transports that bring animals to the north from the south. They are not free. They charge a price to put these animals into a van or truck and drive them to a rescue or adopter in the north. I have not seen what the van or trucks are like but if you can imagine what is it like to be put in a carrier, sometimes just a cardboard box, in a large truck with lots of other

Wren

animals to ride for ten to twelve hours or more. This after being terrified in a shelter or rescue for who knows how long. What condition would they be in by the time they reached their supposed better life?

It is difficult and depressing to see living creatures thrown away like trash day after day. Each one of these creatures has a place in this world and deserves to be loved and to love. So, Wren and Whitaker came to me, along with the lucky other kittens who escaped death to other good Samaritans. Wren and Whitaker were huddled together in a carrier after being driven by a rescue lady, who was in a line of other rescue ladies who helped in their journey. Wren had been spayed, and she and Whitaker were given shots, tested negative for feline leukemia and feline AIDS prior to heading north, and had also been issued a health certificate in order to cross state lines. (A side note: ANY rescue group that brings an animal into another state without a health certificate is not a responsible, legitimate organization).

Once she arrived she was checked out by the vet the in Connecticut. The vet tech did a double take as Whit was in the carrier right on top

Whitaker

of his momma when they examined her. When I took him out of the carrier without his momma he literally trembled. The plan was to try and get Wren into Siamese Cat Rescue and find a loving home for her four-month-old kitten, Whitaker.

Both of these cats were so scared they spent most of the time huddled together under the cat tree. It was mostly Whitaker who huddled on his momma Wren. Wren had that shell-shocked look and really did not react much for the first week or so. I was able to get Whitaker, or Whit as I called him, into a small igloo bed and work on his introduction to humans. He would shake, he was so scared, but eventually he would sit patiently in the igloo bed and let me pet him. Bonnie, a friend of mine and Siamese Cat Rescue volunteer, had sent pictures of Whit to her friend and she and her husband fell in love with this big-eyed scared boy. Arrangements were made for them to adopt Whit. All of us did not know how much progress Whit would make, since he was an older kitten when he was rescued and probably had no human contact prior to

Wren, at home

rescue. We did know he liked other cats, which the adopters had, so we crossed our fingers and toes and waited.

I got periodic reports about how Whit was still hiding in their futon. This went on for weeks, but eventually he came around and, from recent reports, is running the cat show in his home. As you can see from the picture he has grown into a stunning black and white tuxedo cat with his momma's signature mustache.

My job with Wren had just begun. Once Whitaker was gone, she was more in the moment. She would move around the room more, be interested in me while I was in the room, and eventually start to play with me with the string toy. At some point she would jump up on the cat tree and look for belly rubs. I knew she was ready for her new home.

Wren went to live in NH with Carol and Peter, and I got some wonderful pictures of her sitting right next to her dad on the couch. This sweet little girl can unpack her bags because she is home, safe and loved.

— *Barbara G., foster*

The Continuing Story of Whitaker From His New People

Whit was very scared by the time he got home with us and into his safe room, my den. When we went to check on him, we couldn't find him! After a lot of searching, we found him in the arm of the sleep sofa. He'd found a loose piece of fabric and wasn't coming out. We put the sofa on its other arm so we could see him. For the first couple of weeks we'd get hissed at and swatted at if we tried to pet him. He'd ignore the treats I tried to give him, but they'd be gone the next time I checked, as was his food. He never had a problem with the kitty litter. Eventually, he'd stay out of his hiding spot when we came in, though he was wary when we got close. One day I saw him scratch the sofa arm, so several times I scratched the scratching pad and post we'd put in with him as if I was doing my nails. He watched me, and I never saw him go for the couch again.

Whit began to play with the toys we gave him. He would chase a rubber ball when we bounced it but his favorite toy was the ball in the circular scratching pad. We were in danger of getting bitten if we tried to get too friendly. It was not enough to draw blood, so we'd say a sharp NO and I'd blow in his face. It took several times, but eventually it only took a NO with me but it took a little longer with Ron.

I did my usual exercising and ironing and computer work in the den, and Whit started to keep me company. Because of the biting issue, Ron insisted he stay in the safe room until it stopped, but I figured it takes cats to teach a kitten proper cat manners. One day I took the screen door out of the doorway and across the top of the stairs and threw one of his favorite balls into our bedroom. Whit seemed afraid to leave the safe room, but cautiously went after the toy. After that, I could barely get my work done, so I took the screen away from the stairs. I doubt he'd ever seen stairs before but learned fast. I'd throw his ball up the stairs from the living room and he'd retrieve it and insist I throw it again over and over again.

Our two older cats, then-11-year-old Callie, a gray and white "informal" tuxedo, and Eli, a then-5-year-old blue point, weren't so sure about the new kitten. Eli had been upstairs many times to watch Whit through the screen door, but Callie would never go up or down the stairs. Unfortunately, Whit dealt with the older cats with aggression and would chase and go after them so they would hide from him. At one point it got so scary for us I'd begun to think they'd never get along. Thank heavens for the Jackson Galaxy herbals my friend Bonnie Carter lent us while we were waiting for our order to come in. After a few weeks, Eli had enough of the kid and started responding to the aggression. He would flip Whit on his back and beat up his tummy. And Callie started to come into her own as the Alpha cat she'd been before.

Now we agree Whit is the best thing we could have done for all of us. He will never be a lap cat but he does love to be petted when he wants it. At every mealtime he is on his chair demanding love. Several times a day we have to pick up all the toys he's tossed around the house looking for the one he's in the mood for and wants us to play with him. Whit is Eli's shadow, and goes wherever his "big brother" goes most of the time. They take turns chasing each other all over the house and up and down all the stairs, which is more exercise and action than Eli had since we adopted him.

Eli spends as much time as he can out on our enclosed porch. We love seeing all the cats lounging around in there and watching the wild animals outside or soaking in the afternoon sun in the living room bay window. Whit always waits to see if Eli is going to eat when it's time to feed them, and if Eli's not in the mood, or not hungry yet, Whit won't eat until Eli does. Callie now goes up and downstairs as routinely as if she was born to it and has started playing with the toys like never before. She will play with Whit, but a lady has to keep her dignity. She is the Alpha, and one look or a quick whack on the head is all Whit needs to know if she's in the mood.

— *Linda R., adopter*

*Whit, all
grown up*

Jim Bob, AKA Theo

*N*o matter how long you have been doing something you still get surprised with the "smack yourself in the head" moments. Jim Bob (VA 10136), renamed Theo, was rescued by an Animal Control officer in New Hampshire. Maybe he was named after previous rescue people Jim and Bob. First thing I did was change his name as I could not imagine calling this gorgeous boy anything but a name after a teddy bear...a little-worse-for-wear teddy bear.

Theo was an intact male who had survived outside for quite a while and was pretty beat up with many wounds from fighting other males. The vet said he was six years old. I doubt that. I suspect he was more like three. Once he was brought into Animal Control he spent some time recovering from a kitty cold and healing before he even was evaluated by our wonderful intake person, Nancy Roberts. Nancy was just recovering from brain surgery and this was to be her last evaluation. He was evaluated and accepted into our program and his new foster parents drove to New Hampshire to pick him up and bring him to Connecticut. After being at his new foster home for a short time he was transferred to me. Foster Trish had adopted a new fur-family member and needed the space and time to integrate their new wild child Charlie.

Jim Bob/Theo looked like he had survived a war, with dark

Jim Bob, AKA *Theo,*
in foster care

spots on his fur from healing wounds, a scar/gash on his nose and many twisted and broken whiskers. He was angry and untrusting and at that point not predictable. He exhibited Alpha male behavior with a capital "A." It took me a long time to be able to relax when I was with him. The trick is not to show fear but to show your own dominance to an Alpha-type male. He loved attention, but became overstimulated very easily. And yes, both my husband and I got nipped.

As time passed he seemed to settle down and it was time to try to integrate him with my personal cats. That was definitely a no-go since he HATED my boy Dunkin and would attack him on sight. Sadly, Theo was relegated to the foster room. My foster room has a screen door on it, with the bottom half covered with plexiglass. The door is held closed by magnetic clips.

On the day I had to take my 92-year-old mother to a doctor's appointment that lasted five hours. I returned to find blood and fur tufts all over my house. It seemed Theo had pushed the foster room door open and he got the best of poor Dunkin (who is deaf). I put Theo back in his room with something heavy in front of the door and rushed Dunkin to the vet. Thankfully, Dunkin was okay, but it was clear Theo had to be an only.

Theo would call from his room continuously. He was lonely. His meow was little but boy, it never stopped. The screen door now

*Theo,
at home*

61

had a big hook and eye which held it closed even when a BIG cat threw himself at it. It even holds closed with an angry husband complaining "Why the heck did you lock me in?" Whoops!

With time, Theo healed and his coat came in full and beautiful, and his paw pads started to even grow hair. There must have been some Himalayan in this guy. I suspected that when he got home to his family and had the run of the house, no other cats, and lots of attention, he would settle down.

After 169 days in the Siamese Rescue program, Theo's perfect family found him. Theo went home just before Christmas 2014 and has proved me right. He is in home heaven and totally in love with his family and they are with him. He takes turns following his people around the house and gives equal time to each with sleeping arrangements.

PS, my husband misses him and still refers to him as Jim Bob or JB.

— *Nancy R., evaluator; Barbara G., foster*

The Story of Velvet and Bandit

*I*n May of 2004, I received a call from the Animal Control Officer in my town. Helen is one of those rare people that goes out of her way to do the right thing. In the case of cats, Helen has no official right to rescue cats unless they are sick and endangering the public. That said, I have known Helen for 13 years and she has always stepped up to the plate for cats.

Helen was asking my assistance as a Siamese Rescue person along with another rescue person from the area, Lisa.

Jackie was being evicted from her apartment in my town. The health department had made two visits to her home. I was in contact with other rescuers who were trying to find places for all the cats. It was a very stressful situation and Jackie was trying to do the right thing with these cats but still wanted to keep a few in spite of having no idea where she was going. She was very unrealistic.

The living conditions in the apartment were horrible. The ceiling in the kitchen was falling down from an unrepaired water leak the previous winter. Mold was growing down the cabinets All the contents of the apartment had been thrown out, but the smell of male cates spraying and urine was almost unbearable, with strong incense burning in a feeble attempt to mask it.

Our first visit to the apartment was to catalog the cats, getting descriptions and names from information provided by the owner, Jackie, so we could figure who was who. I was to take a female Siamese cat named Velvet and a male Siamese named Bandit (if they could be held) and Lisa was to take two of the other cats that could be handled.

Velvet had been living on top of the refrigerator and ran inside one of the moldy cabinets when we arrived. I was able to get a picture and it serves to remind me just why I do what I do for rescue. No living thing should have to live in that environment.

*Our first meeting
with Velvet*

After trying multiple times to get hold of Velvet, she finally ran under the washing machine and it was obvious I was not going to be able to handle her. She would go with Lisa to be worked with and be adopted out. Bandit was going to Lesley in Massachusetts as a temporary foster, and then to a more permanent foster home in Boston.

On our final visit to the apartment we would try to get the cats into carriers. Most of the cats had had very little handling and several had none, and all were totally freaked out by our being there. Jackie told us that she never really handled the cats but liked to watch them play when they were little.

Velvet had had kittens who all died and she had never gotten pregnant again. Bandit had been handled the most. As we tried to catch the cats they ran towards Jackie's bedroom. Okay, good, we could just close the door and corral them in a smaller area. No, apparently the door had a big hole in it, which had been covered by a piece of fabric. As we tried to catch them they would run in and out through the door and inside the exposed bedsprings of Jackie's bed.

After many attempts, we were able to get Velvet and Bandit in carriers. Lisa was able to get the other two cats into additional carriers. As I said goodbye to the Animal Control Officer it occurred to me that she had to endure the horrible smell of the place which permeated her nose. I bet she got into the shower as soon as she got home!

Lisa and I were off to bring the cats to a vet in another town. We waited at the vet while the cats were SNAP tested and deemed negative for feline AIDS and feline leukemia, and then given their vaccination, which the owner paid for. Lisa took Velvet and two other cats. Bandit went with me. Or so I thought.

That evening I called Lisa, who had taken Velvet, to see how Velvet was doing. She told me that Velvet was doing great. Nothing like what we expected. With a sick feeling in my stomach I called Lesley. I said, "Lesley, how is Bandit doing?" Bandit was hiding up in the corner of the closet in Lesley's foster room. I asked Lesley to look under Bandit's tail. Apparently, "Bandit" was Velvet. I had unknowingly switched them. As they were brother and sister, they were difficult to tell apart. When I called Lisa to tell her about the mix-up she told me that "Velvet" had already been adopted. So, the *true* Velvet stayed with Siamese Rescue and was transferred to another foster mom in Boston, Massachusetts.

After two months with her foster volunteer in Boston, it was clear that Velvet needed further evaluation. She was hissy and defensive when she was approached in her cage. Should she stay in rescue or possibly be transferred to a cat sanctuary where she would live out her life in the company of other cats? Getting cats into a sanctuary like that is not free, so it would cost Siamese Rescue much-needed funds for the other cats in the program. So Velvet was transferred to the Siamese Cat Rescue center in Virginia where she was observed by the director in order to make the right life decision for her.

During the time Velvet was at the Siamese Cat Rescue Center, Bandit's adopter Cathy was discussing Velvet with her best friend Elizabeth. Elizabeth was filled in on what the situation was with Velvet and it was decided that she would adopt Velvet and keep her either in an enclosure in her home or eventually move her into the rest of house with her son. There were many discussions between Elizabeth and the director of Siamese Rescue, and the decision was made to give Velvet a chance at a normal life, so her trip back to Connecticut was arranged.

And so, Velvet came to live with Elizabeth for a time. About six months went by and Elizabeth was making plans to go on vacation to Disney World with her son. She asked Cathy to take Velvet for the week that she would be away. At the time Velvet was still in her cage, so the cage was moved and set up at Cathy's house. Velvet settled in and Cathy allowed Bandit into the room to see if there was any reaction. Cathy was shocked to see that Bandit and Velvet recognized each other. In fact, they tried to get to each other and vocalized quite a bit. This was the turning point.

Unfortunately, everyone had been lied to by the first owner of Velvet. Siamese Rescue had been told that she was spayed, but in fact she had not been. Could hormones have contributed to her behavior? Most probably. Velvet was spayed at Siamese Rescue's expense. The decision was made by Elizabeth that Velvet should remain with Bandit.

The Story of Velvet and Bandit, Part II: Together Again

Velvet remained permanently with Bandit at Cathy's home. Even after nine months apart, they knew each other. Velvet was still very much a project for her new people. She was hissy and growly and continued to react aggressively to her new dad and mom. But they were not going to give up. Again and again, Cathy's husband Rusty would work with Velvet using one of his socks to try and touch her. I

don't have a timeline, but eventually Velvet stopped reacting and let him pet her. As time went on she joined Bandit on the bed at night and slept with the family. They were finally living their life together.

Bandit was Cathy's soul kitty and as Cathy became more and more involved in her rescue group he was the welcome kitty for all the rescue cats that came into her home and then out to their forever homes.

Velvet passed away a few years ago but she had a wonderful loving home and live with her brother and people. Bandit missed her and continued to call for her for a while. He eventually accepted she was gone.

When Bandit became sick a couple of years after losing his beloved sister, Cathy was not going to let him suffer. She provided the best care she could using conventional care and holistic care and gave Bandit an additional year. As tough as it was for Cathy and her husband when it was time for Bandit to go, there was no question that he was going to join his sister.

I find it extremely satisfying that so many of our lives are intertwined by the good we do. The tiniest ripple becomes a wave in the end. changing everything.

— *Barbara G, evaluator; Francine P., foster*

Zeus and the Pills

"Give him the methimazole tuna-flavored chewies," they said. "He'll like them," they said.

Day #1 of getting Zeus to "like" his chewies was easy. He ate it right out of my hand.

Day #2, Zeus decided the tuna-flavored chewie was going to kill him so I had to smash it up in real tuna. That worked...for two days.

Day #4, Zeus decided his chewie smashed up in tuna was my way of poisoning him so he refused to eat it. At this point I felt his mouth was healed up enough (had his remaining rear molars pulled which required some stitches), I could smear his chewie onto the roof of his mouth leaving him with no option—it worked...that day. I tried it again that evening and he growled at me so much and so loudly, Dixie ran across the room and slapped him upside the head. I still managed to get the chewie into his mouth. Thank you, Dixie

Told the vet clinic when I had to refill Zeus's prescription I was going to go with the much cheaper pills. Receptionist told me this always happens. They start cats out with the much pricier treats and cats start to refuse them. I asked why not start out with the more price-tolerable tablets and go from there? The answer was not everyone is like me and capable of pilling their cats. I was flattered so I stopped giving her a hard time.

Day #5 I had a brainstorm. Zeus LOVES his normal kitty treats so I started to smash his chewie meds in between two treats, giving him a treat sandwich. It worked! But I held out little hope this would continue.

Day #7, Zeus decided he dislikes his treat sandwich and the other cats are disappointed, as this also cuts back on their daily treat intake (I don't do regular treat giving—not good for their waist lines.)

Day #8, Zeus seems to enjoy deli chicken and is willing to eat his smashed-up chewie in a bit of deli chicken.

I should have the tablets Friday…I can't wait. The cheap Yankee in me refuses to give up on the chewies until the last dose is into the big guy.

Paul wonders why *his* thyroid meds aren't available in a chocolate pie flavored chewie.

— *Mary P. – Zeus's slave*

Oliver

Oliver lived out of a dumpster in a rent-subsidized apartment complex in New Britain, Connecticut. We don't know how long he survived there, but we suspect he had been abandoned for a long time. A woman who lived there contacted us to ask what happened to him after he had been rescued. She said she had been feeding him on and off for some time. The dumpster was close to an apartment where crack addicts lived and they tormented the cats that were living in the area. It was a sad and horrible existence.

One of our volunteers, Sue, heard about the situation and went to see if she could trap one of the Siamese, hoping he would be a candidate for Siamese Rescue once she got him settled. Little did she know that he was so traumatized he completely shut down when he went into her safe house. She did not know what to expect from him and was a little bit afraid of him and did not attempt to touch him until she could figure him out.

He became a "meatloaf" and sat in her small storage shed in a cage for a month. She spent hours talking and sitting with him to see if she could get him to come around. It was a very slow process with tiny baby steps that were barely perceptible. When it was beginning to get cold, Sue had to make a decision to get Oliver to the vet so she could bring him into the house. He had to get checked out, tested and updated on his vaccines so she would not put her existing house cats in danger.

The first job was to get Oliver into a carrier. We were not sure how he would react to any touching or attempts at corralling him into a smaller place. I went to help her and she was surprised and shocked at my success at just putting the carrier in the bigger cage, door open and pushing him in with a towel covering my hands. Of course, I don't think it would have been as easy if it had been in a larger area. Of course, we had not really examined this boy cat to see what his condition was, so this was a learning experience.

Sue had assumed Oliver was somewhat younger since his coloring was pretty light. Siamese cats tend to get darker with age and in colder weather, with some exceptions. Seal points can get pretty dark in old age. Newborn kittens start out white and get their coloring tips (points) at a few weeks of age. The color continues to deepen as they mature. The lighter-colored Siamese such as chocolate points and lilac points do stay lighter, or can lighten with old age. I think Oliver was a chocolate point but also had been surviving so long outside that his nutrition and health had a lot to do with his coloring.

When we arrived at the vet, we were not quite sure how Oliver would act, but as suspected, he did start to growl in the carrier when the vet technician started to take him out. Because he really needed to be looked over and have some blood drawn, the vet had to sedate him. At first glance we could see he was an old guy. His eyes were marbled, his fur was clumpy, and he had almost no remaining teeth. We were amazed how he had survived. The vet said

he thought Oliver was around 13 years old or older. Oliver passed all his tests and was brought into Sue's spare room, where he remains as a resident of sorts.

In the beginning, I would go to Sue's to visit with Oliver but he clearly did not like or trust me. I have to say I was surprised, because that is not the usual reaction I get since I have so much experience with cats but

71

I respected the feeling. I tend to push the limits with rescue cats to get a feeling for what they are truly like. Sue had made some progress with him and was able to touch and stroke him as he remained under the bed in her spare room. Yes, hours of sitting in the room with him, listening to music, and trying to engage him in play had paid off for Sue, but only slightly. When I would arrive, he would go back to his meatloaf position and be on the watch for any move I made. After I left, it was reported he was back to moving around the room.

It has been a year and I continue to get updates on Oliver's process. He loves to play with an interactive feather, and is now sleeping on top of the bed not under it and the latest report is he is sitting by a window looking out. We don't know what his life was like before he was rescued or even before he was abandoned but he is now safe and even though Sue doesn't know it, he is home.

Duchess

Duchess (VA 9856) sat in a reputable Connecticut shelter for months awaiting a home. She had an untreated eye injury as a kitten, which left one of her eyes cloudy and odd-looking. This was perhaps a turnoff for many adopters, but it added to her beauty for Siamese Rescue.

The shelter felt bad Duchess that kept getting overlooked by adopters and they were thrilled when Siamese Rescue agreed to take Duchess into the program. Her chance for a home was finally here. I found Duchess to be quite playful and she had a bit of a comedienne streak in her. She was fun and full of life; she never let her disability hinder her spirit at all. She played fetch with her favorite toy like no other.

Duchess was adopted by a woman who suffered with Lou Gehrig's disease. There was some concern that Duchess might have a problem with adjusting to life with a person who was wheelchair-bound but she didn't seem to mind that at all. Duchess and her adopter developed a bond quickly.

Sadly, the adopter's disease progressed much too quickly and she had to be placed in hospice. Since Duchess's adopter knew she had this disease at the time of adoption, her hopes were that a family member would take Duchess when she was at a point of no longer being able to care for her. Unfortunately, Duchess refused to acknowledge anyone other than her beloved adopter so it was decided (with the adopter's approval) that Duchess be returned to the care of Siamese Rescue so another home could be found for her.

Duchess was adopted quickly into a home where she has thrived and is as loved as she was before.

Duchess' first adopter did end up losing her battle with Lou Gehrig's disease but she did live long enough to know Duchess had found another loving home.

Siamese Rescue is always there for their "alumni." It was very sad that Duchess lost the first caring home she'd had in a long time, in such a short time. But we were there for her and it sounds like she'll never have to return to us again…but if she does, we are here for her.

— *Barbara G., evaluator;*
Mary P., foster

Sinda

Sinda is a gorgeous blue point wedgie. In rescue we can make no guarantees about whether a cat is purebred, though we believe Sinda is. Along with that comes the very sensitive personality and demanding nature of a Siamese.

Sinda was born to a breeder-hoarder in Connecticut. He was rescued from that situation as a one-year-old cat and he lived with the same family for the next eight years. He lived with another cat, a female Bengal who was older than him. When the family had several children, Sinda became stressed by the activity level in the home and it was reported that he stopped getting along with the other cat. He spent more time on his own, having isolated himself.

He was brought to a shelter where he became further withdrawn. The shelter called us because they felt he would do better in a foster home situation.

Sinda's first foster worked on getting him comfortable and was pretty successful at drawing him out. He spent his days hidden under a blanket at first and would come out at night to play and eat. His former owner reported that he was happiest getting pets when he solicited them. He was a more independent cat and reported to be a lap cat only rarely. His foster mom thought she had found a perfect home for Sinda with a single gentleman who had no other pets. It would only be Sinda and his person. Unfortuantely after two months his new person still could not touch Sinda and Sinda was brought back into Siamese Rescue to try again to find the right fit.

What went wrong? We just don't know, but as Sinda's second foster home I was determined to find out.

Initially, Sinda appared to be quite withdrawn. He would crouch under a blanketed cat tree or inside a dresser drawer. His large ears would point sideways, which showed just how stressed he was with so many changes. At first he would push his nose under

*Scared
Sinda*

the blanket and crawl onto the bed to sleep there all day. When I would not allow him to do that, he would open the dresser drawers and climb inside to hide. I had to remove the largest drawer so it would not fall on top of him. No matter how many times I would close the drawers, he would reopen them. I was thankful he was eating and using the litter box fine after the first few days of settling in.

The key to Sinda was Patience, Patience, Patience. No matter how frustrating it got, time was the cure. It was time spent sitting on the bed watching television while he sat watching me. Time trying to get Sinda to play with the mouse on the wire toy, which would draw him closer and closer, as long as I was on his level. If I stood up, he would quickly run to his corner under the cat tree.

At some point I allowed my personal cats into the foster room to explore. Because Sinda's records said he had stopped getting along with the other cat in his household, I was nervous about his reaction. As I suspected, he just loved the other cats. He wanted to be friends and got right up into their faces, which they did not appreciate at all. My cats were a bit freaked at his forwardness and wanted out of the room immediately. I decided at that point that Sinda had to go to a home with another easygoing cat.

So how was I going to get this cat into a carrier to get his health check done when it was so difficult to handle him? He could not go home without it. It was difficult, but I was able to cover him with a blanket and then grab him and scruff his neck quickly to get him into the the carrier. The next issue was how was he going to be at the vet's office? I was afraid that he would freak out at the vets office like he did when I tried to get him in the carrier.

I told the vet what to expect. She might need a sedative or to use heavy gloves to hold him. Neither were necessary. She had her assistant scruff him tightly and was able to examine him and clip his nails and put him safely back into his carrier. Yes, it often happens that we expect the worst and the worst does not happen. In this case I was very thanksful.

Because there were so many people interested in this very handsame cat, I had to be very careful we did not repeat the mistake of where he first went home. I was very picky on who and where he went. There had to be as little stress in the new home as possible. That ruled out some of his top applicants. The adopter had to accept Sinda as he was in case he did not make progress past being only a cat's cat. There also had to be a best buddy cat that could draw him out.

Sinda at home

The next issue was getting him into a carrier to go home. It was very difficult and I added some war wounds to my already scarred hands and feet. His new person met me at the halfway point to her home. She instantly fell in love, but I was very up-front on his personality. As it turns out, Sinda never trusted me because I proved myself not trustworthy so many times. He had not experienced with that with his new person. He has made good progress in her home. He loves his new sister, and sits on his owner's lap. I have pictures to prove it! While he was with me, he never purred. He is purring in his new home. I think we found Sinda his new forever home. His person, his sister and he are very happy these days.

— *Lisa D., and Barbara G., fosters*

You Are My Sunshine

*S*unshine was a young beautiful flame point Siamese male. His coat was a yummy light orange cream color ("creamsicle"), which was striking with his beautiful blue eyes. He also has amazing little ear tufts at the tips of his ears. Sunshine was named White Flame by the shelter. His first foster Barbara changed his name to Sunshine because he loved to be sung the song "You Are My Sunshine."

Siamese flame point males tend to be pretty laid-back, but because Sunshine had been through a lot in his short life, he was trying to figure out what behavior to choose. Sunshine was given up with 20-plus other cats to a local Massachusetts shelter. He had never been away from his home, which had been with other cats, collie dogs, adults and teenage children. It must have been a pretty busy home and I doubt he and the others got much attention, but we can only guess. He had been dubbed a "spirit cat" by the shelter because he hid most of the time he was in the shelter community room. Barbara felt it was because one of the cats was a bully and would torment him. Sunshine was so scared at the shelter he started to shut down. The shelter would drag him out of his hiding spot to force feed him and give him fluids, but this seemed to make him more scared. Because Sunshine was not eating, the shelter eventually called Siamese Rescue to help.

After arriving at his first foster's house, Sunshine was not interested in eating and his first foster mom intervened by syringe feeding him (easily done) and gave him sub-q fluids. Within a few days he came down with a nasty shelter cold and was pretty sick. It was very clear that this sweet boy was not the "spirit cat" the shelter had labeled him. Once Sunshine was better, he was transferred to my home. (I couldn't take him initially as I was traveling.)

When Sunshine first arrived at my home, he was a very scared boy and would hang out under the futon. Gradually he got used to me and would come out from under the futon to be petted. He loved attention and would roll around on my lap and next to my feet. He was very easily handled and loved to be cuddled. He continued to seek attention but then

would nip (love bite). As he got used to a steady stream of affection this behavior dissipated and his nips became quite gentle when they did occur.

Sunshine made tremendous progress and was given the run of the house when I was home. He could get pretty vocal and would run through the house calling for my cats (three Siamese girls) to come and play with him. They are pretty jaded about fosters and mostly ignored him. If he got too close and invaded their space, they would hiss at him to keep his distance, and he did. He showed absolutely no sign of aggression with them.

While Sunshine made amazing progress, he was still a bit leery of people he did not know, but was usually up and on their laps or next to them within minutes. He was a very vocal guy and called out when he couldn't find you or to remind you that he thought it was time for a meal. I could clip his nails quite easily. He could still be a bit mouthy but understood that a loud "ouch" meant he was being too rough. He loved the Zoom Groom brush and loved to cuddle and snuggle. He was totally integrated with my girls after he had learned what annoyed them. They wouldn't let him snuggle with them but he obviously would if he could. Such a nice cat!

Sunshine found his new forever home with a young woman who was just beginning veterinary school. After much thought about a new name, Sunshine became Simba. Simba helped her cope with the pressures of school by providing comic entertainment and world-class cuddling. Even with a new name, he remains a ray of sunshine.

— *Barbara G., evaluator and foster, and Diane B. foster*

Five Brothers

Jude and Jacob's owner passed away in the winter of 2014, leaving them and their three other cat brothers alone in their home until she was discovered. The animal control officer in Branford, Connecticut seized Jude and his four housemates Jacob, Lazarus, Caleb and Nemo. Because the town shelter was full they were signed over to the vet in the town where all their previous records were held.

Apparently, the owner acquired a new male cat every couple of years. The vet was treating one of the cats for extensive medical needs, and the other cats were behind on their vetting because of the expenses for the sick one. The cats were given full workups including blood tests, vaccines and microchipping. Jude and Caleb had significant dental disease, which was treated by the vet.

Caleb was the last cat into the household and was a very wedgie-style flame point. He was known to be the owner's baby kitty and quite doted on. Emily, a Siamese Rescue volunteer, adopted Caleb, and Jude and Jacob came into Siamese Rescue. Nemo was kept by the vet because he was a "train wreck" in health needs. Lazarus was a very elderly Tonkinese, who, at 18 years old was eventually moved to the vet's home and lived another two and a half years. After a few months I was told he bonded with the vet's husband and liked to sleep on his head at night.

I met Jude and Jacob at the vet's office and was very impressed with how friendly they were to "newcomers" to the office. They had been there for four months. The two boys greeted us and sat on our laps right away. I was able to do their intake evaluation for Siamese Rescue quickly. They were accepted into Siamese Cat Rescue and traveled to Diana's foster home where they settled in nicely.

The first-in-line adopter was a previous adopter of one of my foster cats named Marble. Marble came from a Springfield,

MA shelter and had refused to eat while he was there, common with Siamese cat in the shelter environment. Three weeks went by before Siamese Rescue was called. When Marble went home I suspected there was some serious damage done to his health from his not eating because he died a few weeks after going home to his adopters. He was much loved by the adopters who were crushed by his loss and wanted to adopt again quickly.

The couple went on to adopt two other cats from Siamese Rescue, and then Jude and Jacob. With a new baby in the house all the cats did not mesh. The adopters tried and tried to make it work but it was obvious that Jude and Jacob needed a quieter environment and their own "indentured servants." Jude and Jacob came back into the Siamese Rescue program with Bonnie in Massachusetts as their foster mom. Enter into the picture another couple from Virginia and Karen S., who was their interviewer from Siamese Rescue. Karen had been a longtime friend of mine and a does an amazing job matching rescue cats with their forever families. The planets aligned and Jude and Jacob were to be adopted by the couple in Virginia.

— *Barbara G, evaluator; Diana G. and Bonnie C, fosters*

Following is the story told from Jude's and Jacob's viewpoint. It was a long time coming, but they are where they were supposed to be all along. Their humans cater to all their needs and they receive an abundance of love and laughter back.

Our Story
as told by Jude and Jacob

We're older dudes and had never heard of "mass transit" until foster mom Bonnie put us into a car that was the first part of The Meezer Express caravan. Each car took us closer and closer to our new fur-ever mom and dad. Our new mom calls us "carpetbaggers" because we came from up north to a place called Virginia. That was on March 21, 2015.

When we got to our new fur-ever home, our new mom and dad put us in a big bedroom. Surprise! There was our very own Millie bed on top of the people bed. We were tired and shy so we climbed into our bed to sleep. We didn't feel scared because we had our own bed, plus toys, food, and a special potty—a big tub with a hole cut in the side. (We may be carpetbaggers but we're *not* squatters.) The next morning, we decided to see the rest of our new home. Our new mom thought she was being really sneaky careful when she opened the door but we were ready and waiting and bolted through the door and down the hallway. WOW! It took all day to explore our very own English muffin with so many nooks and crannies. But, by sundown, we owned the place (and mom and dad).

A few weeks later, we met our new doctor. He's really nice and said we look amazing for geezers. Jacob, aka Jake, had to have some dental work. Mom and dad say we are toothless wonders because we eat wet and dry food like champions—especially Jake. Jake reminds mom of humans she doesn't appreciate because they eat and eat and still stay skinny. Well, that's Jake! But mom loves him. She keeps the J&J Mini-Mart fully stocked.

Mom and dad put a special ledge on a "safe" window sill and we spend lots of time sleeping there in the sunshine. Sometimes we sleep in our downstairs Millie bed and sometimes in our upstairs Millie bed. When we aren't sleeping or eating, we play Indy 500, chase Da Bird and the snake wand and chew our cat nip toys. We

also like sleeping on the people bed. We use our scratching posts and play rugs but sometimes Jude forgets and uses the carpet (that's when mom and dad get big voices). We like to sit with mom when she reads and watches TV and we really enjoy using dad's computer keyboard.

Jake says he may run for President (everyone else is). He has opinions on everything and just blurts out whatever he thinks whenever he feels like it. His 4 a.m. filibuster is a specialty mom does not appreciate. Dad just keeps sleeping.

Jude says he has special talents, too. When he wants attention, he puts his paw out and reaches up to say he wants to be held and snuggled. He also curls his paw into a dipper to get a drink of water from a people glass—he especially likes the mug of water on dad's desk.

We 're full of love and big purrs, and that's why we got a special treat—Foster mom Bonnie, her husband (Uncle Earl) and God-mommy Karen (our interviewer) came to visit us. That was such a special treat. We think they're special for finding us the best mom and dad we could ever imagine. The caravan people are special, too. SCRC is good. Our life is very good.

Purrs,
Jacob and Jude

Hi everyone,

Jude and Jake here: Wow! We can hardly believe it has been one whole year since we came to live with our fur-ever mom and dad in Virginia. A while back, we woke up and it was snowing and snowing and snowing. We thought we were back in Massachusetts but mom told us we are still in Virginia and it was just a big Virginia-style snow storm. She told us to climb up on our window ledge and enjoy watching snowflakes fall down because Virginia doesn't get so much snow like Massachusetts. Whew! We were so happy we were safe and warm inside with our food and water and treats.

Jude here: I've been practicing new table manners. Now I like to use a front paw to scoop food and water up into my mouth. I practiced using the mug of water dad keeps on his desk. He's okay with sharing his water with me. He also keeps a bag of treats in one of the desk drawers. We try to be really quiet but somehow Jacob, who has radar ears, comes running and demands his more than fair share. Jake thinks everyone should share everything with him. Sometimes, mom and dad call him "jealous Jake." Not to be outdone by dad, mom also keeps a bag of treats in a desk in her tv room. Shhhh! Don't tell dad. We sure have a great life. Treats here, treats there, treats, treats everywhere. Oh, one more thing about Jake—sometimes he isn't nearly as clever as he thinks he is because he goes into a room, pushes the door closed, then screams like a banshee because he can't get out. Mom says he's simple.

Jake here: Since I've been on grain-free food, I've had only a few upset tummy episodes. I still eat like a competitive foodie but don't get sick now. Sometimes Mom and dad give us a spoonful of shredded baked chicken or salmon or grilled steak and those are really awesome treats. Recently, I discovered that mom makes an outstanding Millie bed substitution when she sleeps. I just climb up on her hip, settle in, and we're off to dreamland. I don't share that spot with Jude. Jude likes to sleep next to mom pushed up against her arm. Oh, and I am NOT simple—I just know how to get attention.

Jake and Jude: When Mom is doing stuff around the house, we like to visit dad in his office—we're really good at sorting papers and we're learning to use the computer. We also like to sit with him in his recliner where we all watch TV through closed eyelids. Not wanting to play favorites, we then go upstairs and sit on mom's lap while she reads or watches TV. Mom says all four of us are geezers so we're going to move to a retirement community nearby. We get to take all our toys and Millie beds, our mini-mart, our special litter box, and our TREATS. She says it will be a good place where we will all still all be together but we won't have to go up and down stairs. So, all-in-all, we've had a terrific year. Here's looking forward to year two.

Mom and Dad here: We are blessed!

Respectfully submitted with purrs,
J&J

March 21, 2017

Hello everyone!

Amazing! Can you believe we were adopted two years ago today? Neither can we but it sure has been a fur-bilicious two years.

We have everything we could hope for, including a big new Malcolm bed we got for Christmas, along with some new afghans and toys. Our Malcolm is mostly where we go when a human lap isn't available. We're sending pictures from Christmas when we were figuring out our new Malcolm bed. So, okay, our sunny window bed is another favorite place and we still sometimes use our Millie bed. When we're not sleeping and sunning, we like to sit with mom and dad when they work at their desks. Jude watches the coffee cups and water glasses and, when the time is just right, he dips a paw in to get a taste (or two or three or four). Jake is not as subtle—he just sticks his whole face in and starts gulping (he flunked Siamese Finishing School.)

We had our six months checkup at the doc's place. He says we are doing great for a couple of Meezers. Everyone there, including our terrific vet, says we are very handsome and ever so well-behaved. Mom has to give Jake some Pepcid every day because he has a very sensitive stomach and has throw-up accidents. She mumbles about someone named Stanley Steamer but then she hugs him and tells him she loves him. Actually, she says that a lot to both of us.

Mom told us we are still waiting to move to the old folks' home but we're not worried. She said because we are Meezers and they are geezers, we are all going to stay together and she promises lots of sunshiny windows and all our stuff will have top priority.

We still send greetings to our foster family (Aunt Bonnie and Uncle Earl) and our coordinator Karen and her two girls (Cara and Coco). So, life is good and we know we are two very lucky boys.

Whisker kisses,
Jake and Jude

Hello everyone!

We decided to share what's been going on in our lives the past few weeks.

Once upon a time, you remember, we were taken on a loooooong ride from Massachusetts to a place called Virginia. Back then we were learning about the Revolutionary War because our foster dad is into all things Revolutionary War. When we got to Virginia, we thought maybe we would see soldiers in gray and soldiers in red, empty tea tins, muskets and horses (we still miss our Llama from when we were in Massachusetts). After all that travel, we decided to give the new people and the new digs a fighting chance. So, it's been two and one-half years and we love our people and our house where we get lots of food, water, beds, blankets, toys, and chin and ear scritches. Mom and Dad keep telling us they love us a whole bunch (whatever a bunch is). So, everything was going along nicely until...

About two months ago, these people came in OUR house and started nosing around looking in rooms and closets and even the bathrooms. Those nosy people went away but showed up again and kept looking all around. We decided we better put some hedge around our bets so we played nice with the woman just in case.

Well, the very next day, another woman showed up with a fist full of papers and we don't know what all that was about except she kept mom and dad at the dining room table for about three hours. Seems those nosy people wanted to buy OUR house before it was on what they kept calling "the market." Since we didn't think they were referring to the farmer's market, we started getting really nervous. So, we sat at the top of the stairs keeping one eye on the table and the other on the closet where our carriers are stashed.

Next thing was some woman that mom doesn't like came with some papers and told mom and dad all the great things she would do (for a big bunch of money) so we began to fear for our food allowance. A few days later, a man shows up with a clipboard and HE walks all around our house making marks on his clipboard. He talked about how a junk truck could be provided. JUNK TRUCK? Well! We made record time getting to our litter box. Junk truck? Seriously? Mom! Dad! We're not junk! We're your very own sweet and loving boys!

So, now we get to about five weeks ago. Two nice ladies showed up with a whole big bunch of cardboard and tissue paper. The ladies put everything in the paper and then in the boxes.

Then came Monday, August 21—a really scary day for us. We were put in a bedroom with our stuff so all we could hear were bumping and thumping noises. What could be happening? Our home was being invaded. All these guys came rushing around and they took all our stuff out to a really big truck. They took

EVERYTHING! EVERYTHING EXCEPT US! Okay, so they didn't take dad, either.

So, there we were, alone with dad in a totally empty house. All that was left were our carriers, blankets, food, and water dishes. Where was mom? Did she get put in the big truck? We started to feel sad and scared.

About four hours later, dad's cell phone rang and he said "Okay boys, we're going for a ride." Yikes! A ride? A "ride" means one of two things: a visit to our doctor or we're going to a new home and new humans.

BUT WAIT! We needed to start thinking positive thoughts and positive thinking helped. We got to ride in the new car—nice! And, as we rode across a river, dad said we were almost to our new home and everything would be fine because mom was waiting for us. Better and better with every turn of the wheels on their axles.

Dad carried us into our new home. It had new smells and sounds but we were together with our mom and dad. We saw all our familiar furniture, our food dishes, our customized litter box, the big basket with our toys, our afghans, and our mom. Sigh!

We've been together in our big new apartment for five weeks. Everything is lovely. Mom and dad say we're real troopers and we adapted just like good Siamese boys. Another life adventure has begun.

Life isn't so bad at the old folks' home. Not so bad for older people. Not so bad for older Siamese, either.

Respectfully submitted,
Jake and Jude

Sometimes You Just Need
A Leg Up in Life

*M*id-October 2017 I received an email from a very reputable NH shelter that an approximately two-year-old stray Siamese cat had been found wandering about the city.

This cat needed immediate amputation surgery due to a nasty large cancerous tumor taking over her left front paw.

I quickly emailed an intake evaluator to get to the shelter to evaluate this cat in order to get her accepted into Siamese Rescue. I then called my vet to set up a tentative appointment for the amputation.

Due to the medical needs of this cat, the shelter did not do the normal seven-day stray hold. Time was of the essence for this one. So young, so sweet and trusting—it seemed she had wandered about just looking for someone to help her.

When a Siamese cat is in need it always amazes me how quickly our volunteers will respond to offer assistance. I was first contacted about this cat on a Thursday and by Saturday morning she was at my house, with surgery scheduled for that following Tuesday.

As it turned out, the day before the surgery, the shelter received a call from a distraught person looking for her *thirteen-year-old* Siamese cat. Her major distinguishing feature was the large tumor on her front left paw.

Fortunately, having just started a new job, I was scheduled to go into work late that morning so I was able to start my rather frantic phone calling.

First to Siamese Rescue's director, to update her as to the events. Since the shelter hadn't done the stray hold due to the medical needs of this cat, legally we had no right to hold the cat. I called the cat's owner (I was able to find out the cat's name was Suki) and we made arrangements for her to come get Suki the following day. I did impress upon her the severity of the tumor and the need for Suki to get immediate medical care for the tumor. Due to the nature of the tumor—it was a fast-growing one—it would not take long for it to affect her heart and lungs.

Other than the nasty tumor overtaking her paw, Suki was in great physical shape. Everyone, including the shelter vet, thought she was much younger than 13. Her teeth were pearly white with pink gums; her claws were the thin sharp claws of a much-younger cat. I was floored when I found out her age. And she was very sweet, very loving, and very friendly. I could only cross my fingers that her owner would do right by her.

Two days after Suki went home I received a call from her owner that her vet quoted her a very high price for the surgery, and being a single parent to an active teenage son, she couldn't afford the surgery. She wanted to surrender Suki to Siamese Rescue so she could receive the medical care she urgently needed.

I called Siri, Siamese Rescue's director, and she offered to call the owner. A few minutes later I had an email from Siri letting me know that Siamese Rescue was going to pay for Suki's surgery and Suki would stay with me a few days in order to heal, and then she'd go home.

One of the requirements, in order to foster for Siamese Rescue, is to have a vet clinic that is willing to work with rescue on pricing. Siamese Rescue always meets the medical needs of the cats in their program. But in order to do this the cost of vet care is critical. My vet offers great pricing options to rescue. The cost of the surgery was quoted at half of what the price was given to Suki's owner by her vet.

Yes, vet clinics need to make money to stay in business; but when they price owners right out of being able to take care of medical emergencies, what happens to the animal? Many of us know.

So, Suki returned, and I didn't mind because she was a wonderful cat to care for. She had her surgery, and four days later

was returned to her grateful owner. (Who, in turn, managed to scrape up enough money to pay for half of the surgery.)

I was proud to have been a part of this, even if I almost hoped Suki's owner wouldn't show up to get her! I could easily have kept that sweet little Meezer.

— Mary P., foster

Rudy's Story

*I*magine being purchased from a breeder with your littermate sister, and living a happy, fun, good life.

Imagine your beloved person passing away and then you not only lose her but you are taken away from your sister, never to see her again.

Imagine having to get used to a new home, a new person and then *that* person passes away.

Now you've not only lost your sister but also two people, and find yourself once again in a new home with three other cats you've just met.

You find you like your life with those three cats but then your new person passes away and the man that keeps you ignores you for the next three years.

When that man dies you are put into a shelter and labeled aggressive. All you can do is lean against the wall of the large bathroom you are placed into and refuse to acknowledge anyone or anything. Whenever anyone tries to touch you, all you can do is hiss and growl. You keep your eyes closed with fear—fear of what is going to happen next.

But you had your lucky day, dear Rudy (VA9982), because even though the shelter labeled you aggressive they didn't want anything bad to happen to you. Fortunately, they knew about Siamese Rescue and contacted me.

I went to visit you—you hissed and growled at me when I moved but what I saw in your eyes did not say aggressive to me… your eyes were screaming, "Help! I don't know what to do."

I didn't bring you home that day and I'm sorry I had to make you wait another week. But that following week I went to see you again and you had already placed yourself in your carrier. I brought you home and let you hide for a few days. Once I had a

better understanding of you I carried you around my house in a homemade sling and I could feel your little heart pounding in your chest. You weren't ready to trust yet but you let me handle you.

An adopter (your true rescue angel) saw your potential, and when she came to meet you, your first reaction was to slap your possible new meowmy. She stepped back and said "I can see I probably pushed him too hard too quickly, but I want to offer him a home." I figured if your hitting her didn't scare her off, she was the purrson to help you onto the road to recovery.

Your adopter is what we like to call an Adoption Angel. Your new family has given you all the time you've needed to overcome all of the heartache you suffered in your short life; and best of all they adopted another Siamese Rescue Meezer to give you (and her) a friend. This little girl readily accepted you, as you did her; and you have become a big brother again.

I'm glad I could read you on that first visit. What is often mistaken for aggression quite frequently is fear. You wore your heart on your sleeve, dear Rudy, and it saved your life.

I saved your life and your new family made you part of theirs.

— *Mary P., evaluator and foster*

Rudy Update

Rudy has made major strides. He displays his happiness by showing off his body language and expressions. He shows more inquisitiveness and hangs around in the common areas more, even positioning himself to stare at me. He is cleverer than one could imagine and has less anxiety now after a few years.

— Johnna, Rudy's adopter

Allsa, AKA Harvey

Siamese Rescue volunteers try to stay up to date on cats that are at the shelters. Sometimes the shelter contacts us and sometimes they don't. In Allsa's case the shelter called one of our volunteers to come see him. This cat was on the edge of starvation. Harvey was a 13-year-old seal point Siamese who came into the shelter October 1, 2016. The shelter notes said he rarely ate and was given appetite stimulants and fluids. He had come down with a shelter cold and the shelter was giving him doxycycline (antibiotic) for several weeks which further upset his stomach. Allsa was terrified at the shelter. Our volunteer Sue found him way in the back of the shelter on the bottom level cage where you could hear dogs barking from another room. It was clear that Allsa was on the way out of this life if we did not get him out of there.

Allsa obviously lost his owner and his home but the shelter did not know the circumstances other than he was surrendered by a couple saying he was a stray. The staff saw enough surrenders to guess that they knew this cat.

Sue was able to get the shelter to release him to her and we found a rescue person to keep him safe until we were able to either get him into Siamese Rescue or find him a permanent home.

Allsa at the shelter

Allsa was frightened by the ride to his temporary foster home and the new environment, but he quickly made significant strides in craving attention and also started eating on his own in about 24 hours and after one syringe feeding by his rescue caregiver.

Thanks to Mary P. who contacted a previous adopter of one of her fosters, Rudy, Allsa found his new home. I drove with Sue to meet his new forever mom part way to his home. He was not very happy in the carrier. Sue and I were nervous but hopeful that Allsa was going to his forever home. We knew nothing about his past experience with other cats. Did he get along with other pets or did he need to be an only? We did know he was a purebred modern-style Siamese cat so probably would be more on the needy and people interactive side. Allsa was renamed Harvey by his new family and they quickly fell in love with his loving personality.

The next step was integration with the other cats in the house. We know from experience that most of the time integration has to be done slowly. Rudy and Leah were not so thrilled at first. Things seemed to go smoothly until all three cats came together in the dining room and Harvey attacked Leah. No one know for sure why, but of course the new family was extremely upset and discussed returning Harvey to his foster home. After much serious discussion it was decided to give Harvey an extended probation period to see if things could work out.

It was noticed a day after the traumatic event that there was a catnip pouch on the floor of the room where the cats had fought and it was thought maybe it had something to do with the catnip. As a rescue person I have had a few cats who became pretty aggressive or what I call "mean drunks" after playing with catnip, and maybe the integration had been done too quickly. For the time being Harvey was kept in a separate room with one of the owners sleeping with him at night and visiting him during the day. Leah was still recuperating and wouldn't be able to run or walk well if she needed to, so time would tell.

After additional time and a slow integration, Harvey, Leah and Rudy now get along great. Harvey and Leah even spend time sleeping together in different areas of the house. Harvey has gained over two pounds and continues to be loving and interactive with his new fur-ever people. I think the family can't think of a time when the trio had not been together.

— *Dorothy D., and Sue D., rescuers; Johnna adopter*

Leah and Harvey at home

Mojo Rising

*I*n the spring of 2015, Mojo was found in North Carolina among fourteen other kittens. All were malnourished. Siamese Cat Rescue volunteer Julie rescued Mojo and he was eventually placed with his wonderful Siamese Cat Rescue foster mom Michelle in Tennessee. After a month with his foster mom he was ready to go home.

Mojo's new home was with a nice lady who worked from home and would be able to spend a lot of time with him. He was happy. Just a month later, and at about 17 weeks of age, Mojo's life changed. He had a horrible accident. The adopter's family had come to visit and were instructed to keep the home safe for the kitten. Ignoring this request, a family member left a window open. That night Mojo fell out of the third story window onto concrete. Nobody knew until about 5AM when it was noticed Mojo was missing. My stomach aches for that five-hour period that this boy lay alone, injured and scared, in and out of consciousness. After a frantic search, he was found and brought to an emergency vet. According to the initial vet report, Mojo's front right leg was painful and non-weight bearing. His rear right leg and pelvis were also potentially fractured. There did not appear to be any spinal injuries and Mojo was alert on presentation to the vet. The adopter was told that Mojo needed treatment or she would need to elect humane euthanasia.

The call came to Siamese Cat Rescue the next day and they stepped in to help. We are a rescue family and cried and prayed for one of our babies. Mojo's front leg needed to be amputated as it was beyond repair. His rear leg was set in hopes of saving it.

After two days of oxygen Mojo was stabilized and his leg was amputated. His rear leg was put in a splint for six weeks. Mojo, a

*Mojo before
the accident*

previously active kitten, now barely five months old, had to spend
the next six weeks lying on his side, being carried to the litterbox,
and being hand fed. But he never lost his spirit. I cried for him
often during this time, and I know many of the Siamese Cat
Rescue volunteers did as well. We got updates from the adopter
telling us that he was trying to figure things out. He had gone from
a confident kitty to a scared and jumpy boy. His adopter worked
day and night with him to let him know that he could trust his
environment again. Mojo was sad, but his spirit was never broken!

Six weeks later, Mojo's splint was removed. The good news was
that his leg could be saved. The bad news was it had been set wrong
and could no longer be repaired. It was set straight out, pointing
to the rear. Mojo was back to stage one and had to relearn things
again. Since he had already spent so much of his life in a cage
while healing, his adopter decided to let him "figure it out" and
learn with what he had. Mojo was a champ during this time; he
conquered his disability. It was now the end of September and the
beginnings of Mojo's life as a three-legged boy.

Mojo started to settle in. As a rescue, we do not hear much
from the adopter at this point. A few months later Mojo's adopter
contacted Siamese Cat Rescue about returning him. Due to
personal reasons, she could no longer give him the care he needed.
Sadly, this boy who had been through so much, who had completely
bonded with his one and only person, was going to have to go

Mojo all grown up

through more changes. He would literally have to leave the person whose hand had fed him and whom he trusted. When I heard the news, I cried for him all over again, I was mad and sad. Foster mom Michelle was also angry. She wanted him to come back to her for foster care, but Mojo was quite far. It was decided he would go to Jackie, the closest foster, in order to get him back into the Siamese Cat Rescue program as quickly as possible.

I knew right away that I was interested in adopting this boy. I needed him. I asked my husband Mike about it, but he said "NO!" After a day of the idea settling in, he started to reconsider. Mike saw that Mojo had a place in my heart, so it was not difficult for Mike to agree that we needed to bring Mojo into our home.

When Mojo arrived at Jackie's, thanks to the help of the Meezer Express, he was angry and sad. He hissed and growled, then purred and headbutted, then hissed and growled. Jackie got to know him a bit and was able to share with us what Mojo would need in his next home. Basically, he needed stability and unconditional love. We have that, so we were the lucky family that got to adopt this wonderful special boy!

A few weeks later Mojo traveled to us on the Meezer Express. Mojo took almost three months to integrate into our home of three cats. Now they live happily together. Since his arrival, we learned quite a lot about this boy. Mojo always has an opinion, and is sure to let us know, especially when it's time to eat! He has a sensitive stomach, so any alterations to food makes for a not-so-fun few days of litter box cleaning. Mojo is a real trooper and never lets his limitations stop him; he doesn't even know he is different. Sometimes he is a bit klutzy, but he always gets a big hug from one of us if he has a little mishap. He is a carbo-holic, so we now must keep all breads hidden or he will break through the bag. Mojo is an over-groomer, has very thin hair because of it, but that continually is getting better since he is now truly a part of the family. Mojo will sleep right between Mike and me on our pillows, we love it! He knows he is home, he knows he is safe. He loves having other cats in the home, and loves being part of our family of six people and four cats.

— *Monique O., Mojo's forever mom*

The Snowshoe Sisters

*I*t is a Saturday afternoon and I am sitting at my laptop typing away while Sweet Pea sits in the cat tree on one side of the room and Cassie sits up on the dresser top beside the TV on the other side of the room. The girls are my new foster girls and are a bit standoffish. I don't blame them. They were given up when their person had to move to an apartment to downsize. The apartment complex would only allow two cats. Sweet Pea and Cassie's cat mom and dad were chosen because they were older. The girls had lived in this home all their lives and never had been to a vet. Both of them were very tiny. I thought the adopter had to be wrong on their age of five years, because they looked to be older kittens. Sweet Pea weighed 5 pounds 10 ounces and Cassie weighed a mere 5 pounds 4 ounces. They were way underweight.

After getting permission to bring them into Siamese Rescue they were brought to the vet immediately to be spayed and given their shots. This consisted of three vet visits: one for the initial SNAP testing, another to be spayed, and then a return to check the incisions and give them their updated vaccines. Of course, they are not feeling so great recovering from the surgery and shots and

Sweet Pea

having total strangers handle them. I am waiting not-so-patiently for their true personalities to come out as they settle in.

Days have gone by and I continue to wait for these two girls to realize they are safe. I can pet them for a few minutes but then they get very nervous and will swat and nip. They are eating and using the litter box, but someone's tummy is upset. Is this why they are reacting to me? It is anyone's guess. I was told they were a bonded pair, never having been separate from each other and their parents. Now that they are spayed, has it changed the dynamics? Would it be better to separate them into different foster homes so one does not feed off the other's nervousness? Sweet Pea is the more dependent of the two. Would she do better bonding with a foster parent instead of the constant hissing at her by her sister? I will wait and see if I can settle their upset stomachs first before I try to make any more drastic changes for the girls.

Sweet Pea and Cassie have now been separated a few days. I do believe Sweet Pea is doing much better without her sister's hissy presence. Cassie was clearly miserable and you could feel it by just being in the room with her. Sweet Pea is now enjoying playing with the feather toy and chasing it like crazy. She comes to me to give head butts and is purring and talking softly. She would love to be outside the room, but is intimidated by the presence of my cats who are not to receptive of her. Sweet Pea is turning into a sweetheart of a kitty. Updates on Cassie from her

Cassie

A more relaxed Sweet Pea

new foster mom are all good as she continues also to make strides in her new foster home.

Sweet Pea is putting on a little weight and becoming more interactive. She comes to be petted, and headbutts me, makes bread and purrs up a storm. We have long play sessions with the feather string toy and I get tired before she does. She is now sleeping next to me on the bed in the foster room, which I count as major progress. I still get a nip once in a while. But It has been a month since Sweet Pea arrived and she has come a long way. I have started letting her out of her safe room for short periods of time and she is doing well with my boy kitties. If they get too close she puts them in their place with a hiss and a pretend swat. Unfortunately, my female, very loving greeter girl Millie is not so nice to Sweet Pea. Millie is quite jealous of Sweet Pea and will try to follow her around the house very closely. This tends to make Sweet Pea and me very nervous. I have to supervise the two of them very closely.

Now I just have to wait for Sweet Pea's forever family to discover her! She will be a wonderful companion to her person and another laid-back kitty. Someone will be very lucky.

— *Sue D., evaluator; Barbara G., foster*

Newbury

"Older than dirt"...that's what we said about her.

Newbury (VA12259) was found as a stray on city streets in July of 2017. It was a hot July and the thought of this declawed elderly Meezer, with a mouth full of bad teeth, being alone was heartbreaking. Even more so when we realized how severe her condition was.

Newbury was in renal failure, and due to lack of nutrition her muscles had somewhat atrophied. She had one paw she wouldn't even step on. She walked on the hock of that paw. She wobbled and weaved and couldn't stand up straight. In spite of her condition she was approved for intake with the knowledge that she was most likely a hospice situation. But, in spite of her condition, Newbury remained loving and trusting. I can't imagine, nor do I like to think about how rough things had been for her.

Originally Newbury went to a foster in Massachusetts, as I had a foster in-house. Once that cat went home Newbury came to stay with me in New Hampshire.

Newbury had to be given sub-q fluids daily and it was difficult to get her to eat well. I started to feel that we weren't doing anything to improve her quality of life, we were only sustaining life. And I couldn't help but wonder if that was fair to her. I consulted Siamese Rescue's director, wondering if it was time to let Newbury go. It was suggested to have her blood panel redone and go from there. If her kidney values were no better, euthanasia would be considered.

The surprise came when we found out Newbury's kidney levels were showing signs of improvement; the key was going to be finding a food she would eat. Since she ate so little, she did not have regular bowel movements. This poor cat would only defecate about once every three days. I knew she had to eat more, and in spite of the daily fluids for hydration, she simply needed more nutrition.

Siamese Rescue's director mailed me a box of various wet foods to tempt Newbury's palate. Lo and behold, she liked one type. She ate it every time I offered it to her and we got to the point where she needed fluids only every other day, then every third day as she was starting to remain hydrated. But alas, she still didn't move her bowels on a regular basis.

Newbury was even looking better and was starting to react to her surroundings. When she first arrived she'd lie in the bed and accept all of the attention she received. Once she started to eat better she would slap my dog and hiss at my cats—a sure sign she was starting to get some gumption back! She was starting to act like a diva sealpoint girl. Loved it!

One Friday night we noticed that Newbury really didn't want to be bothered. Once she had started to eat better, Newbury had claimed my husband's lap as her own, but that Friday night she didn't want anything to do with him. She wouldn't eat and only slept. In my heart I knew something was up. I'm pretty sure Newbury was making her choice. I think she was done fighting the good fight and had decided to retreat.

I woke up that Saturday morning and found Newbury had passed during the night. As sad as it was I knew her body and spirit were tired.

I was always happy to have been able to give the old girl a few weeks of care and love. She was off the city streets and into a home that was willing to care for her as long as she wanted that care. She passed away safe and warm.

Newbury was my first hospice foster, and in 14 years of fostering for Siamese Rescue with over 100 Meezers having passed through my home, she was the first one to pass away under my care.

But you know, it was worth it just knowing she went to Rainbow Bridge loved.

— Chris M., evaluator, Mary P., foster

Peter the Cat

I loved my two-legged Mom. I really did. You see, she saved me from the life of an outside barn cat, and that is no life for a handsome Meezer boy!!

I was really young when my Mom came to get me. We were happy together and she took very good care of me. Then our lives turned upside down.

Mom had some people helping her but they took advantage of her and perhaps were not so nice to me. When my Mom's family found out, they stepped in to help and got her the care she needed, which meant going into the hospital and then rehab. When she came home they felt it was too risky for her to have me winding around her legs trying to help make her feel better. So, they put me in the basement temporarily. They did actively seek a better situation for me but things just weren't working out. I was only two years old and I really missed my Mom! She was all I knew, and suddenly she and I couldn't share our adoration for each other anymore. I cried and cried but nobody would listen to me.

Luckily for me, they did stumble across Siamese Rescue and worked with the intake volunteers to get me into a new home. A new home that wouldn't be basement living.

When the intake volunteer came to visit with me I was so happy to have understanding attention. Barbara played with me and loved on me. I showed her that I'm a really good boy and that I missed being someone's center of attention. And because I'm such a handsome seal point Meezer with a sweet personality, Siamese Rescue took me in.

Right now, I'm at Foster Mary's house awaiting my new home. I know I'm going to get one because Foster Mary told me I have about nine approved adopters who really want me—ME! They want me! I'm just hanging around waiting for Foster Mary to make

sure my potential forever home is going to be the right match, and I need to have a dental before I go home. I have a couple of bad teeth that need to be dealt with.

Although I was scared, lonely and depressed being in that basement, things are look up for me. I'm sure my first two-legged Mom is happy knowing that I'm safe and getting lots of attention; and that my forever home is just a few weeks away.

Like so many of the Meezers taken in by Siamese Rescue there is a sad story...but a happy ending!

— Barbara G., evaluator; Mary P., foster